Is the
United States
Worth Saving?

For a more perfect union!

Charles W. Thompson

"Contentedly we say it will always be. No! No! You will lose it – and if you lose it here, all the world loses!"

Common Sense, Thomas Paine

IS THE UNITED STATES WORTH SAVING?

This book is written to provide information and motivation to readers. Its purpose is not to render any type of psychological, legal, or professional advice of any kind. The content is the sole opinion and expression of the author, and not necessarily that of the publisher.

Copyright © 2019 by Charles W. Thompson

All rights reserved. No part of this book may be reproduced, transmitted, or distributed in any form by any means, including, but not limited to, recording, photocopying, or taking screenshots of parts of the book, without prior written permission from the author or the publisher. Brief quotations for noncommercial purposes, such as book reviews, permitted by Fair Use of the U.S. Copyright Law, are allowed without written permissions, as long as such quotations do not cause damage to the book's commercial value. For permissions, write to the publisher, whose address is stated below.

Printed in the United States of America.

ISBN   978-1-949746-85-3   (Paperback)
ISBN   978-1-949746-86-0   (Digital)

Lettra Press books may be ordered through booksellers or by contacting:

Lettra Press LLC
18229 E 52nd Ave.
Denver City, CO 80249
1 303 586 1431 | info@lettrapress.com
www.lettrapress.com

ACKNOWLEDGMENTS

No one ever accomplishes anything worthwhile entirely on their own. This is certainly true in my case. I will first acknowledge my mother who encouraged me to read, to never give up on a project and to respect all people. Certainly there were several university professors to whom I owe more than can be easily expressed – opening my consciousness to what education and democracy means to humanity. Next, my wife, Luz Maria, without whom there would have been a much lesser result; she encouraged, critiqued and made many helpful suggestions. I am indebted to Dr. Terry Timmins of Orange Coast College for several meaningful suggestions and his encouragement for my efforts. I owe Mrs. Carmen Smith a vote of thanks for her suggestions and to Theodore J. Gotsch, retired administrative law judge, thanks for his comments and information on chapter 3, "To Ensure Justice". Finally, without his knowledge, President David Boren of Oklahoma University who inspired me to write this book when I read his book "A Letter to America".

Charles W. Thompson

Huntington Beach, California, 2013

To my children

Charles Randall
Craig Jonathan
Linda Leigh

Contents

Acknowledgments v
Foreword xi
Introduction Is the United States worth saving? xvii

Chapter 1   Why is the United States Worth Saving? 1
Chapter 2   To Form a More Perfect Union 22
Chapter 3   To Establish Justice 44
Chapter 4   Insure Domestic Tranquility 61
Chapter 5   Provide for the Common Defense 71
Chapter 6   Promote The General Welfare 88
Chapter 7   Secure the Blessings of Liberty to Ourselves and
            to our Posterity 109
Chapter 8   Our Bill of Liberty 120

Epilogue 127

"I know neither North nor South; I know only the Union ….. In politics I am an old fogey, because I cling devotedly to those primitive principles upon which our government was founded."

Sam Houston quoted in "Profiles in Courage"
By John F. Kennedy

FOREWORD

Why am I writing this book? First, it is my love for my country and being devoted to the cause and blessings of liberty. Since early childhood I have wanted to serve in some capacity to benefit society. Secondly, my personal creed and ambition is to leave this world a better place for having had the privilege of being here. The third reason is I am a firm believer in the concept of a republic as outlined in the constitution's preamble. Finally, I have lived long enough to witness our nation in very good times and have benefited from those noteworthy times. Regretfully, I have also witnessed a breakdown in democratic governance.

Having studied government and economics and having served government in a professional capacity in four states over a span of four decades, I have witnessed the decline in representative government. I have seen congressmen, elected from gerrymandered districts pursuing their public trust pandering to special interests without a worry or concern about major issues or being reelected. I have seen congressmen who appeared more interested in personal pleasures and garnering as much personal wealth as lobbyists – favor seekers – could provide them.

I do not wish to leave the impression that the scene has been totally bleak. There have been many well-intentioned representatives who have endeavored to bring about positive public policy. Some have been disillusioned in the process; it is an arduous task to get meaningful improvements adopted but many of them keep trying. It takes a herculean effort to make changes that are critically needed in our time. Foremost among these needed changes is to wake up to the fact that current issues today cannot be treated as if we are still 13 colony states – a mindset that defies 21st century reality. It is essential to accept and address the reality that serious complications abound for the continuance of republican rule.

From all that I have observed and studied in my lifetime, it is my conclusion that our representative system needs a modern overhaul to meet 21st century requirements. We must force political parties to serve the public interest and compel those who represent the people to become responsible to those who elect them. We must develop ways and means to hold political parties responsible to their words and we need to update our representative system to better represent people rather than tracts of land or campaign contributors. We need to reinforce our judiciary, find a way to utilize the nation's intelligence, develop and maintain the world's best public educational system and take a very, very serious look at our social values.

In the pages that follow I have endeavored first and foremost to make a case to update our constitution, bring concerted public attention on our social mores and present some provocative ideas so that we might realize the benefits of a true republic, not only for ourselves but for our posterity. We owe this not only to ourselves and our posterity but to those early colonists, who at great personal sacrifice gave us independence from monarchy. Do we ever think about, realize and appreciate what those early Americans gave us?

The freedoms we enjoy we owe to our founding-fathers who gave us a Constitution the likes of which had never been known in the history of humankind. I still wonder with amazement how they did it against all odds. I wonder if we have retained the devotion to liberty and self-government and whether the passion for liberty and freedom still flows in our blood veins. Will we, can we, maintain and enhance what they entrusted to us or will we squander it as the prodigal heir?

IS THE UNITED STATES WORTH SAVING?

In my zeal to present a case for the continuance of liberty, opportunity and an improved society, it is possible I may have gone too far for some people. If this is the case please accept my apologies, ignore those parts and concentrate only on fundamental ideas to improve the framework of a new republic. My objective has been to arouse Americans to the debasement of democratic practices, to the growth of poverty, the diminution of our "middle-class" and how the slow, almost imperceptible erosion of the republic is occurring year-by-year.

Also, it is my hope and fervent wish to motivate all citizens to think about and participate in our governance and consider their individual importance in a free society – no chain can be stronger than its weakest links. These are issues on which all true Americans and believers in democracy should be able to find ways to reach agreement for the benefit and welfare of every one – no exclusions.

There can be no question that our constitution has provided a beacon of freedom to the world for more than 200 years. And there is no question that we now live in a totally different world compared to colonial America of 1789. The 18th century way of life is gone forever and our focus must be upon 21st century reality. My wish is that all Americans, those with a devotion to liberty, will unite for the single purpose to insist on constitutional corrections to guarantee liberty, justice and opportunity for the next two centuries – an enormous task but no greater than what our forefathers accomplished against much greater odds.

All of us should emulate Sam Houston who knew only the union – not just some part of it. It is only our union that has made America great. We are Americans – we live where we want to live, North, South, East, West or to the mid-Pacific or to the subarctic. Do we continue to have someone like that lifelong Southerner who sacrificed his career trying to stave off a civil war – a far greater cause than winning the Battle of San Jacinto, capturing a Mexican general and winning independence for a Republic of Texas.

There are always numerous problems and difficulties to be faced in order to accomplish any great and worthwhile goal – the status quo will not yield easily. But the barriers which will be encountered will exact a far lesser sacrifice than the loss of our liberties and self-governance or the loss of a beacon of human freedom for the world to see.

Every citizen needs to present their views to those in political office and never fail to follow-up to check for results – concerted citizen action is a powerful force. Let us never accept piecemeal efforts as a response, as a crumb for our efforts. To achieve the fundamental corrections in our governance will require prolonged and determined effort, all worthwhile goals exact a price – liberty has already cost human sacrifice in uncountable numbers. Our sacrifice will be measured by the strength of our devotion to democracy.

Charles W. Thompson

We the People of the United States, in Order to form a more perfect Union, establish Justice, insure domestic Tranquility, provide for the common defense, promote the general Welfare, and secure the Blessings of Liberty to ourselves and our Posterity, do ordain and establish this Constitution for the United States of America.

Is the United States worth saving?

An introduction*

> "If men were angels no government would be necessary"
> James Madison.

This treatise directs itself to the dangers America faces in losing representative government and to propose some ideas to improve and perhaps save our republic. If our republic is to be saved we need to be provoked into taking meaningful steps to address obvious deficiencies in our present governmental practices by getting a clear picture of what our governance is today compared to the intent and purpose as expressed in the Declaration of Independence and our Constitution's preamble. These are our founding values which define our national purpose, those ideals which bind us together and to which we pledge allegiance–values which our Constitution is expected to implement. We must never lose sight of our founding values.

What our present generation can contribute is the fundamental question of our time. Consider that totalitarian regimes are on the rise and that

---

* Throughout this treatise the words "republic" and "democracy" are used interchangeably to mean the same thing – representative government – without regard to their technical difference. In addition the phrases "republican form" of government and "democratic form" are used interchangeably to connote the same thing as they seem best to suit the text.

the vast majority of people in the world now live under autocratic or theocratic governments. We can't afford to wait for a new generation to correct problems which we have passed along to them, if indeed the opportunity still exists!

What is at stake in saving our American government? The answer is actually in our hands today, in our determination to correct, to improve and to reinvent a modern republic – to save the best efforts that have ever been made by mankind to form that more perfect union. Let us ask ourselves whether our attitudes and our actions coincide with our dedication to liberty. If there is a major disconnect then our way of life is indeed facing dire problems.

Stop to consider that our founding fathers were men of substantial material wealth as well as being predominant figures of government. Then seriously ask why would they sacrifice "their lives, their fortunes and their sacred honor" for the belief in and hopes to form a republic? Are there any senators, governors, congressmen or major CEOs who would do a similar thing today?

There is a fundamental question which confronts us: which is more important in our lives, a republic or the economy? Both are indispensable but we must decide whether we live to work or do we work to live. In the socioeconomic order, one or the other will predominate. Facing reality, if our goal is democracy, then the economy must be in harmony with republican principles. When the economy controls government policy it becomes corporatism and rights become subservient to that cause. At issue is whether democratic principles and ideas or vast amounts of money, derived from unknown sources, will dominate state and national governments. If our mission is to preserve our liberty and the rule of law then we, the people, must find ways to reclaim control of "our" government.

The United States must now thrive in a world unknown and undreamed of by our constitutional framers. They knew of a laissez faire economy which had little to do with public governance of that day. Since that time our economy grew into the world's largest producer and now it has mutated into a part of a world economy. The result is that we are now faced with two basic choices. One is to become a pseudo-republic, dominated by multinational business interests with unlimited financial resources, with supremacy over a class divided society. Predictably this future would lead toward hybrid corporatism under our present constitutional framework – or a sort of pseudo-democratic oligarchy.

The remaining choice is to amend our constitution to guarantee true representative government, develop our educational system back to world prominence, and using the intelligence we have in our national institutions, to explore ways and means to improve our lives in order to realize the American dream. We can do this by correcting our course toward a true republic. We should not fail to recognize and comprehend the vast differences between the two choices.

The challenge is to seriously and honestly ask ourselves whether we really want to live in a democracy. Should the reply be affirmative then be prepared for the follow-up question: what are you going to do about it? How this question is answered actually answers the first one. Are we capable, as a society, of intelligently determining and designing our republic as our constitutional framers did? The alternative is to just go along with things, oblivious to a fast-moving world and let things happen as they will. Does such a decision sound like a sagacious, thoughtful response? Our republic will not persist under such conditions.

Such a venture inevitably introduces the necessity to question our social mores, our economic practices, as well as our political governance. We must candidly consider what makes us what we are and intelligently consider what we want to be. Only when we know and can define what kind of society and what kind of government we desire and demand can our goal be made clear and achievable. When the goal is in sight all actions, programs and proposals can be assessed as favorable or detrimental to that goal. Let us with open minds investigate some ways to reach the goal of a true republic.

We must question the rights and responsibilities of the individual as well as how our governmental structure and arrangements protect and serve us. What new legal arrangements can realistically be made if a new birth of freedom is to be realized? To achieve this it becomes incumbent upon us to face issues, without bias, endeavoring to put aside preconceived political and economic preferences which will allow us to examine new arrangements to meet changed requirements and conditions of a new age. Our forefathers were not encumbered by being brainwashed by numerous "isms" and focused on one concept, a republic. Are we capable of emulating their performance without regressing to some favorite ideology, "ism" or dogma? We must concentrate on one ideal – a real, true republic.

Reason varies with each person, no two are exactly alike. What a person's senses identify and is available to be integrated, is unique to that person. No two people will ever totally agree on everything. All public decisions, when they are needed to be made, must of necessity be compromises. Since every human being is a unique creation there are no "universal truths" in the political world. This fact becomes fundamentally important when applied to how we should live together and how society is organized and how an effective government can function in order to serve and respond to everyone.

It is only in a society where individual freedom is a fundamental right, to the extent that everyone's fundamental right to freedom is protected also, that human imagination, creativity and the pursuit toward fulfillment can flourish and progress. That kind of society will always demand justice, equality and opportunity. Perhaps, there can be general agreement on these tenets.

To ask or assume that life long held opinions and preconceived beliefs regarding political, economic, religious and social issues could be set aside is highly improbable. Endeavoring to set aside only our political opinions, however, and to consider other ideas, which possibly may be best for our nation, should be worth the effort. When we think of the future and seriously consider what is at stake, the very future of democracy, we will realize that such an effort is the right thing to do. Let our patriotism, our devotion to human liberty, for justice, for opportunity and a common aspiration for a true republic be the guide to our reasoning and action.

During the past two centuries since our constitution was adopted we have witnessed the most profound advancements and changes in human circumstances in history. The vast majority of these changes have occurred in the last three quarters of a century. Our generation has witnessed the greatest changes and alterations in the way people have lived during the past century than occurred during the previous 7000 years! This is 21st century reality! There has never been a time like this before and we are the ones who must deal with it. Has our thinking, our mindsets, kept pace?

The economic system of the 13 colonies is no longer realistic. We are 180° separated from that bygone day. Free, unfettered economy was possible when people knew who the producer was – in those days the producers were real craftsmen who took pride in what they did. Laissez faire economics was an appropriate economic practice then but as antiquated as the horse and buggy is today. The economy of 1789 was never a factor in governance to our constitutional framers.

In the beginning of our nation there was no real concept or reason to think of a dichotomy in which the people's government and how the people made their living were to be separate functions of the social order. Our founding fathers neither intended nor did they make any provision for such a separation in the Declaration of Independence, the Constitution or in the writings of the Federalist papers. In the Declaration of Independence, however, they did include an acknowledgment that the rights of man were endowed by our Creator.

We should stop and consider why so many people from all over the world and of every ethnicity and religion on earth want to come to America. This unprecedented and prodigious outpouring of people's yearnings speaks to the universal nature of humanity and its need and desire to be free, to seek opportunity as well as to be secure and safe. These are goals which are fundamental to all mankind and they were, in fact, among the reasons which propelled your ancestors and mine to come to America – that is, unless you happen to be an American Indian. Have we become so accustomed to liberty that it is now taken for granted? As citizens born in a land of freedom and opportunity, do we enter society accepting and taking it as a birthright for which nothing is owed or required?

Our republic, to which we ceremoniously pledge allegiance, which has been entrusted and bestowed upon us, has come at a very dear price. Nothing has come easy. Our constitutional framers had their acrimonious debates but managed to reach conclusions even when many proposals put forth dissatisfied many of the delegates. Now our goal is to provoke unfettered thoughts and ideas toward addressing 21st century reality. The objective is to preserve and reinforce democracy which could be as enduring as the one we have inherited. Isn't it true that what we really want is a true democracy, not just for ourselves but for posterity? Everyone wants and strives for freedom, opportunity, safety, justice and good health because they are basic human necessities!

It is essential to accept the fact that nothing of human construction is perfect nor can it perpetually endure. We are in a world that is in a state of constant change and change affects society, economic systems, as well as our governance. Obviously we should never view human creations as unchangeable or so venerated that they should last forever. The Constitution of the United States, together with its 27 amendments is a case in point. We are rightfully inspired by the perspicacity of its framers but no one, even the framers themselves, considered the document to be perfect – it required 10 amendments, just to achieve ratification. Constitutional amendments reveal our endeavors to progress toward that more perfect union.

Time and growth, cultural modifications, worldwide economic changes, an evolving society and experiences along with a vast array of technological innovations have brought a plethora of unforeseen challenges since 1787. Recognition of these changes in the world around us points clearly to the necessity to adapt to these changes – all have an impact on how we live, how we govern and what is required to protect and maintain democracy.

IS THE UNITED STATES WORTH SAVING?

The tendency to take a dogmatic, self-serving and authoritative posture toward any single issue will prove unproductive in our efforts to improve our governance. It also defeats our purpose of enhancing and improving democracy not just for ourselves but to serve posterity for the next two centuries. A doctrinaire and inflexible attitude could also be a sign of mental rigor mortis and it contributes what that characteristic implies.

Our republic will always be formulated on the criteria listed in the Preamble of our Constitution. It is for us, in our time, to expand the innate meaning of the preamble to meet 21st century requirements and circumstances. Their meaning is far more than basic organizational titles for they express the very purpose for which the revolution for independence was fought. Our constitution is our written definition and the formula defining the means and methods to bring meaning of the preamble to fruition. The preamble clearly states what a republic is meant to accomplish.

The beliefs, customs and practices of society will have considerable and significant impacts on our governance. Is the ethos of our nation congruent with our professed belief in democracy? The wide disparity in the social practices and lifestyles prevalent in our country today stem from many constituent causes. No one can question the wide chasm in the diversity and circumstances of people. The basic purpose of a republic is not to change people but rather to provide them with ways and means to productively utilize freedom in order to maximize their potential and to provide opportunity under the rule of law to achieve it. Under such circumstances those with the determination and talent will receive their just rewards.

We human beings are far from perfect. Our first president, George Washington, warned us "it was a rare man with virtue enough to resist the highest bidder." Greed, avarice and chicanery will most likely be a troubling human condition for many years to come if not always. An improved democracy will not solve or answer all these conditions. But through education and national standards, directed toward our social mores, we may be able to alleviate the most excessive of such abuses. Is honesty too much to require, to demand, in public affairs?

Would society and the overall human condition become better for everyone if education, basic life necessities, health, and opportunity were equally available to all? Many will reply that such an egalitarian concept is unrealistic. However, before subscribing to that position, recall that our forefathers bequeathed to us a formula for a republic, and a republic, a government of, by and for the people, is an egalitarian concept of governance. We have added 27 amendments endeavoring to reach the goal of a republic but we have yet to perfect our objective.

Few if any worthwhile goals are easily obtained, it is a step-by-step process to achieve that more perfect union. Unless we continue to strive to achieve it, its un-attainment will be assured and Montesquieu's hypothesis would appear to be upheld. He maintained that republics, with only small homogenous societies, where culture and ethnicity were essentially the same, could survive over time. Or will we agree with Madison's rebuttal? He argued that a heterogeneous population with cultural diversity required a republic, allowing everyone to be heard and to pursue their preferred lifestyles, to successfully govern over time.

In a democracy there should be the assurance that an equal opportunity to succeed is a right available to all. It should be noted that personal preferences regarding professions, or vocations, and the public's perceived importance attached to them, varies greatly and has consequential impacts on the acquisition of wealth. Should great wealth be the leading determinant deciding the life's work of people? Is it the only incentive for greater endeavor, for invention and innovation and for happiness and human progress? Should it be the principal or only factor which receives public acclaim? What are the factors which actually improve and advance the human condition? Can we develop productive and beneficial answers to such questions? Our social mores reflect what the people currently deem acceptable and which have highly significant impacts on how our nation progresses – may we never minimize their importance.

Can we face the truth about our national circumstances? Or do we prefer to ignore the bad and assume that the good parts tell the entire story? How much do we really care? Seriously consider the role that society's value system plays in how we live and work, what we strive for and devote our time and resources on. In today's America, from a social standpoint, what is considered the prime mark of success in life? Is it a vocational aim to improve the human condition, to pursue a path for self-improvement, to discover and build new things, or to seek good times or garner as much wealth as possible? Our value system drives the nation!

Pause and consider which vocations contribute most to society and to the human condition. Does the welfare of society depend more upon teachers, doctors, nurses, skilled craftsman or a host of other talented and highly competent commercial entrepreneurs than it does to movie celebrities, professional athletes or heads of giant corporations? If monetary rewards are the answer then we would have to say that the latter is the obvious choice of society. The entire latter group does add interest and temporary enjoyment but to what degree do they advance the human condition? What has been the result? Which will affect our tomorrow's for the betterment of society? Does our value system tip in the right direction when placed on the balance scales? It is critically important that we resolve to formulate plans for improvement for our future. Are there ways to begin improvements in our societal values? We will delve into some of the aspects of these questions in the sections that follow.

Where on the scale of importance does our society place education, the acquisition of material abundance, public health, religion, family or personal contributions? What we know from history, as well as from biblical accounts, is that hedonistic societies do not last. A balance must be found which places emphasis on both personal and societal improvement. Obviously there will be many different views to these questions. The questions, however, should cause all of us to consider where our true values should lie. What is vital to a democratic society is to consciously know and select what is valuable and most necessary and try to live accordingly. To do otherwise is to continue to proceed along a path with an unknown terminus.

There are many questions for which realistic solutions need to be found to further our pursuit of that more perfect union. The formation of our social mores evolve from many factors including parenting, neighborhood environment, education, theology, avocations, entertainment and the way we make our living. The test of a great society is finding a way to improve in all these areas of human activity. To arrive at satisfactory answers, given today's social norms, is likely to be a formidable objective in the near future but assuredly worthy of our best endeavors to pursue. Over time small steps will have great impact. To paraphrase an adage, if we don't take the first step we will never complete the journey.

We became the first nation in history whose government was purposefully designed to form a republic. It was humanity's first attempt at self governance designed to escape medieval concepts of control by the "divine right of Kings". It was also the first declared attempt to escape the tyranny of sectarian religious rule and to permit people to worship according to the dictates of their conscience. Theocratic rule has never permitted individual freedom, but freedom imposes critical responsibilities on each individual to exercise that freedom carefully, with thoughtfulness and accountability.

It is now our chance to enhance and transmit a better democracy to posterity than the one we were born into and to which we pledge our allegiance. As a society intent on governing itself, we must not fail to be aware of and to address our standards and practices of social conduct for they are the realm of our existence. In the last analysis they reveal what kind of people we are and provide and direct the course we will take in the future.

Another fundamental requirement for our success toward improving our democracy is to realize and accept the fact that all people are intrinsically the same. Biologically we are virtually identical regardless of geographical location, race or ethnicity. Our differences are a result of tens of thousands of years of geographical separation, climatic conditions, diets and culture that have shaped variations in human physiology and culture. We should celebrate our differences for it guarantees variety which in turn provides interest, growth and progress. No culture has ever possessed all the right and best answers to life and living conditions. To preserve and reinforce our democracy there is a need to revitalize our social contract based on total membership in order to offer a life worth living for everyone – democracy is not the exclusive domain of any select ethnic group.

The ancient republics of Greece and Rome offer lessons to alert us of the dangers of slow, imperceptible developments which erode individual liberty. Upon such a review we see some general similarities to our situation. Internal strife and cultural decay always played a role in their demise. Their history reveals alternating swings from tyranny to anarchy interspaced by brief republican rule revealing the ascendancy of human traits to gain power and fame above devotion and belief in democracy. Commonly, there was a divergence from their founding principles which played a significant part in their ultimate failure.

The more recent history of Italy reveals how it evolved from democratic rule to corporatism and to totalitarian fascism and its eventual partnership with Nazi Germany. Also consider the reasons why the Soviet Union collapsed. Chief among the reasons were overexpansion into countries which did not want to accept their governance; Soviet leadership came to realize that communism did not work; they became nearly bankrupt trying to cope militarily with the United States; they failed to recognize and accommodate the many and varied ethnic groups with vastly different cultures, language and history – and the private ambitions of those who sought power and fortune led to bitter internal divisiveness. Throughout history similar reasons have caused the decline and collapse of many regimes. Does any of this provide any lessons for the United States today?

In view of these histories we must realize that as difficult as it may be to make major reforms in our governmental system it will certainly be easier to do so before power becomes so invested that only by public uprisings can meaningful corrections be made possible. Let us not force our posterity into that remedy.

Today, as we consider our founding principles indelibly emblazoned in the preamble of our Constitution, we realize that none have been fully realized. This is a call to re-examine their meaning and intent as they apply to 21st century America. History and current events scream out to us to take notice of how slow, gradual change and internal strife alters and destroy great empires. Failure to recognize these changes threaten our republic and must be addressed before it is too late. Their accumulative effects on government are dangerous and daunting problems while individually, curiously, many changes go unnoticed and unrelated to their effects on government. Over time as small alterations to democratic practices are ignored or excused they may be even championed as custom!

Consider the influence of money on political campaigns and ask yourself where this money comes from. Do those who give vast amounts of money expect anything in return? Does the recipient owe any allegiance to the donor? Does this depict true public representation? Does the exercise of common sense tell us to take action while we can to make the fundamental improvements that are required to propel the new republic through and beyond our century?

There is a prologue of our constitution's preamble found in the Declaration of Independence which every American should memorize: "We hold these truths to be self-evident that all men are created equal, that they are endowed by their creator with certain unalienable rights, that among these are life, liberty and the pursuit of happiness. That to secure these rights, governments are instituted among men, deriving their just powers from the consent of the governed, that whenever any form of government becomes destructive of these ends, it is the right of the people to alter or to abolish it, and institute to new government laying its foundation on such principles and organizing its powers in such form as to them shall seem most likely to affect their safety and happiness". Do we need more direction than what the Declaration of Independence advocated and our constitution's preamble proposes?

Our endeavors must focus on the real needs and aspirations of all our people and we have a time proven formula to do it. It becomes necessary to delve into what our forefathers brought forth as an objective and the framework to achieve their expectations for the new government. The foundation they left us was expressed explicitly and inspirational – "in order to form a more perfect union, to establish justice, to insure domestic tranquility, to provide for the common defense, to promote the general welfare and secure the blessings of liberty to ourselves and our posterity". These are all the directions we need to understand and fulfill their injunction to gain the aspirations which can be realized in a true republic. These are our founding principles.

Stop and reflect on these criteria which spell out the purposes for which our nation was formed and what it was meant to accomplish. The preamble not only stipulates the purposes for which the Constitution was written but sets forth the very conditions which are necessary to form and maintain a republic. They become the foundation on which to build and maintain a democratic society. All laws and governmental practices must support and be harmonious with these six criteria.

Isaac Newton told us that his insights came from building on the advances made by others. And it was Benjamin Franklin who, in reply to the question regarding what the constitutional framers had done, replied that it was a republic "if we could keep it". We are the generation that must follow Isaac Newton's advice and accept Benjamin Franklin's challenge. Is it not for us to "nobly advance" our republic? Are we bold enough to reinvigorate a quest for democracy and ensure that our republic endures? Comparatively our quest should be easier than that of our forebears since we are not now required "to pledge our lives, our fortunes and our sacred honor." Perhaps, only our honor!

These six objectives form a template by which the new republic could not only be constructed but continually updated and improved. They represent the purpose for which the remainder of the constitution is meant to achieve. They set the parameters around which proposals for all future improvements are to be gauged. The constitution is the building, the preamble is the foundation. As time, knowledge, national and world situations change the building is likely to need remodeling but our founding principles must live on and to them we must remain true.

After an unequivocal experience of the inefficacy of the subsisting Federal Government, you are called upon to deliberate on a new Constitution for the United States of America. The subject speaks its own importance; comprehending in its consequences, nothing less than the existence of the UNION, the safety and welfare of the parts of which it is composed, the fate of an empire, in many respects, the most interesting in the world. It has been frequently remarked, that it seems to have been reserved to the people of this country, by their conduct and example, to decide the important question, whether societies of men are really capable or not, of establishing good government from reflection and choice, or whether they are forever destined to depend, for their political constitutions, on accident and force. ….and a wrong election of the part we shall act, may, in this view, deserve to be considered as the general misfortune of mankind.

Publius – The Federalist I

CHAPTER 1

Why is the United States Worth Saving?

"Things do not get better by being left alone. Unless they are adjusted, they explode with a shattering detonation." Sir Winston Churchill, "A Churchill Reader" edited by Colin R. Coote.

Is the United States worth saving? We might assume that the answer from a vast majority of Americans would be a resounding "yes"! But assuredly there would be numerous replies with innumerable exceptions. Possibly there could be a meager few who would voice a negative response or would feel better with a lesser egalitarian society.

We can be assured that when any substantial group of people come together individualism will be present. The great differences found in people in their preferences of life styles, their attitudes and concepts to seek opportunity, safety, and freedom reveal our diverse characteristics. However, everyone seeks and fundamentally agrees on a society which assures them the prospects for all these attributes which are plausible only in a democracy! This is the kind of America worth saving. The question is whether the vast majority of American citizens are finding what they seek and how their aspirations can become more feasible in the years ahead.

These personal differences concerning many facets of social and individual life guarantees a variety of opinions and approaches to political and socioeconomic matters. It corroborates the fact that human thought cannot be controlled. In the history of mankind no dogma, no ideology, no religion has ever been conceived to contradict this truism – there will always be dissenters on virtually any issue. However it should be noted that this trait, on occasion, has been the harbinger for reform and betterment. But meaningful dissent requires informed and appropriate ideas which are compatible with the ideals of a true republic. To rephrase Ben Franklin, only when one frees themselves from excessive ego and feelings of hostility towards others are they able to more accurately see things as they are, and in so doing, arrive at a conclusion to doubt somewhat one's own infallibility. This kind of dissent becomes an open window to progress. Ideas evolve to meet requirements and questions concerning personal circumstances, living conditions, national issues and the unknowns of the future. Some exploration of conditions in our society and governance could help save the world's best attempt at democracy. The know-how is available, is the will?

In the course of human history many different attempts have been made to govern the great disparity inherent in people. Many tyrannical rulers have held control through the use of military power but few have outlasted the leader's lifetime. The only viable governmental form to successfully govern over time in a complex society is a republic, where all views can be made known and progress can be made through compromise. It was James Madison who assured us this would be true in his defense of our Constitution. [Federalist Papers X]

Since the advent of the printing press and the subsequent growth of public education the world has witnessed a slow, steady development of governmental ideas to institutionalize binding social contracts to allow individual liberty. The growing realization that all people are the same in their desire for freedom, for opportunity, for safety, for good health and for social equality has been the great transforming agent in world affairs during the past two and a quarter centuries. This is the march of human history. Education has been the key.

IS THE UNITED STATES WORTH SAVING?

We live at a unique time in our history – a crossroads when our nation faces political and socioeconomic confusion regarding how to proceed. One path points to a form of corporatism under the Constitution. The other returns us on our journey toward popular democracy. We live at a time when course corrections are imperative if our republic is to be preserved. We live in a time when economic activity rules our lives and a decision must be made whether our lives are meant to serve the economy or whether the economy should serve society. We live in a new era where action must be taken to accommodate what growth, science, technology and practice has produced in order to preserve our republic. Failure would not only be a misfortune for us but a major misfortune for mankind.

During a time of such political and social confusion an opportunity exists to emulate our founding fathers and remodel our republic for the 21st century. Can we find a James Madison, a Benjamin Franklin, a Alexander Hamilton, a George Mason and, perhaps, hope for a George Washington or maybe a Thomas Paine?

Recall that it was a similar time when our new independent states, under the Articles of Confederation, found themselves at a critical crossroads where a decision had to be made to remain as 13 sovereign nations or to become the United States of America. When interstate trade squabbles arose and an anemic government could not respond it took Shay's rebellion and a general concern that anarchy would soon prevail to demand that something had to be done. In 1787 that something was the Constitutional Convention in Philadelphia where 55 exceptional men, 18 of whom were veterans of the Revolutionary War, produced one of the greatest documents in the history of mankind – the Constitution of the United States of America – a clear remedy to solve the chaos of that day.

Have we produced public spirited citizens today who believe so fervently in human dignity and liberty, who can set aside partisan politics, personal ambitions and through selfless endeavor bring about those vital course corrections required to ensure the continuance of our republic for another 200 years? If our objectives are clear and well-defined to achieve a more perfect union, prospects of success become possible, because the cause is right and just.

As we attempt to correct the problems we face it is essential to keep in mind that nothing is ever accomplished if all objections must be overcome before action is taken. The authors of our Constitution were keenly aware of this fact and most were not convinced of the excellence of their work. All of the signers made compromises. They knew that they had put forth the best effort they could to formulate a republic. For more than 200 years we have continued to make progress. Today we are faced with the necessity to revitalize an ailing republic and renew our legacy of "the land of the free" by utilizing a ready-made framework to build on – the preamble of the Constitution. To achieve its meaning is all we need for a guide, five conforming principles for republican government which are necessary to form a more perfect union.

To confront this situation head-on we must ask ourselves some penetrating questions. Are there conditions, practices, situations or circumstances in our governance that degrade or diminish representative government? Are there some conditions which we do not want to face or admit? Let us take an unbiased look at some features of our society and try to factually appraise the situation.

Consider a society where about one person in six lives in poverty and are very apt to be neglected in the educational system. That translates into having more than 42 million people trying to live, as a family of four, on less than $23,500 a year. We have a House of Representatives where 80% of the membership come to office from gerrymandered districts and our population contains some 30 million people who have no means for healthcare.[*]

We are a nation where tens of thousands of children drop out of school annually. We live in a society where less than 10% of the people own more wealth than the remaining 90% and where the 400 wealthiest families own more wealth than 50 million of the poorest families. In

---

[*] This has subsequently been addressed by the National Affordable Care Act

2007 nearly one half, 49.7%, of the total income of the nation was received by 10% of the population. This resulted in one of the biggest income distribution gaps in US history. Ironically this distribution of income was virtually identical to the distribution of income in 1928, the eve of the Great Depression!

Consider that this same society spends more money on incarceration and prisons than it does on education and has more people in prison than the total population of a score of other nations. Only a half century earlier our society boasted the world's best educational system and is now ranked below 15 to 20 other nations in several educational fields. This is the same society where numerous highly trained youth now seek employment in other nations – a 180° turnaround from just a decade earlier. Surely these are not the arrangements that we wish to save. We have many problems and we have many great strengths among which is a moral compass that has always pointed to "do what is right" – we know that such conditions are not what democracy and social morality should accept.

Medical science has proven that the DNA of all people is essentially identical and that regardless of visible differences all people are biologically the same. We are bound together inextricably also in our belief and concern for the preservation of our republic. We all want and seek the same things – safety, equality under law and freedom to pursue our lives in a peaceful manner, the opportunity to better ourselves and to worship as the dictates of conscience compels. Our nation was founded with one of its principals being freedom of religion. Zealots of all faiths have, at one time or another in history, either attempted or introduced theological governments. None have succeeded. We must never allow the wall between church and state to be broached which would allow our democracy to become a theocracy and an end to personal liberty. Our quality of life and our future depends upon uniting behind common goals consisting of personal choice as a way of life. By so doing we become capable of great things and will continue to be that nation which others will want to emulate.

Don't dismiss as an idle warning the possibilities that determined groups may be able to insert their will through devious intrusions into state and federal laws. Collectively there are groups in this nation which spend many millions of dollars every year trying to remake America in their – not God's – image. Their program consists of attempts to censor books in our schools, the introduction of studies of their theology in public schools, in short, they are saying do it their way – and only their way! This is the way of all theocratic regimes. When only one belief system prevails, whether that be a theology or socioeconomic doctrine, we need only to look at others who have tried it – Hitler, Stalin, Mussolini and now we are faced with Iran, China, Cuba and North Korea. They have all failed or they will fail because they try to limit the innate characteristics of human beings to think. Freedom of thought cannot be legislated.

Our nation is a shining example of how people, left to their own devices, will continue to strive for a better life. Throughout our history we have had several periods during which the general public enjoyed noteworthy conditions. There have been numerous periods of reasonably acceptable conditions and there have been too many times when large numbers of people were destitute. Our economy has always had its highs and lows, the boom and bust cycles. All of these times exhibited the characteristics of how the nation's income was distributed and how our nation's monetary system was utilized, i.e. misused. In spite of this there is been a continuing effort through democratic means to find answers to these fundamental problems of our society.

Money was devised by mankind as a more convenient medium of exchange. Since this early beginning money has evolved into a commodity itself – money is wagered – some may say speculated –in myriad ways and when one wins, many others lose. The manipulation of finances is not capitalism. It is more like Russian roulette – there are more empty chambers in the speculator's gun but sooner or later a bullet is loaded in the firing chamber. When this happens panic sets in and most of society suffers the consequences. The larger and more widespread these wagers become the greater the impact on people's lives.

IS THE UNITED STATES WORTH SAVING?

The economic debacle of 2008 was far worse than the American people realized and how the banks, Wall Street and a large number of those connected with the housing industry, perverted the entire national economy – and bilked the American taxpayer. When management of the financial system is altered to speculate it deviates to an aberrant, self-serving institution only for its own enrichment. It should serve as a medium for economic growth and as a public service for society which guarantees its value.

Speaking about managing a nation's monetary system and banking, legendary economist Paul Volker had this to say "….. Here we are faced with the worst economic crisis since the Great Depression; and whether there really is a sense in the marketplace that something is going seriously wrong – I'm not sure that that attitude is even there. A different side of it is the amount of money spent on lobbying, the amount of money spent on elections, all of which effects the political process. It is a little discouraging, I put that very mildly." Adding.….. "It is a reflection of the fact that there has been a loss of discipline among what is right and natural and ethical. How can you rely on the banks to set rates when the banks themselves are the measuring stick?"**

Money must be managed to serve public requirements, not manipulated to enrich a few who have gained control as if they created and owned the nation's medium of exchange. Monopolistic results in banking must be controlled by breaking up the largest financial institutions. Let competitive enterprise show the way. Consider the fact that the nation's six largest financial institutions control assets in excess of $9 trillion, an amount close to 2/3 of our gross domestic product [GDP]. Shouldn't the first consideration be the nation's interest? Today these financial institutions serve to enrich a few individuals as opposed to targeting the hundreds of thousands of small businesses, the real economic engine of our nation. Small, free, and competitive enterprise, businesses create more jobs than the mega international corporations. We must insist that the Federal Reserve Board is, in practice, a true public watchdog and

---

** Newsweek – Sept 24, 2012

manager as the safeguard over the nation's monetary system. It must be divorced from control by Wall Street.

When the nation's (and the world's) economy rests heavily on our monetary policies do we dare not have a failsafe arrangement to control and manage it? The financial debacle can be defined in a brief description – greed, unethical and unprincipled practices induced and driven by the prospects of riches.*** It was Ralph Waldo Emerson who said, "Man is a god in ruins." That description clearly implies an inescapable need for complete control of the medium of exchange.

Money must serve the public welfare – uses for which it was intended. Utilization of money must follow well formulated rules insuring that productive endeavors, legitimate entrepreneurism, home ownership, and other appropriate individual public needs to shape and serve individual social and economic purposes.

Consider that "by 2008 over 10,000 hedge funds managing more than $2.65 trillion" along with other creative asset innovations this amount swelled to where "the value of assets created and traded on stock, bond and derivatives markets exceeded the economic output of the entire world."**** Is this true capitalism?

We live in a society of vast differences and a world characterized by change –a concept easily acknowledged but very difficult to fully comprehend. Vast economic and social changes pose a grave threat for democracy requiring timely solutions if our republic is to survive. We have grown up hearing from school, newspapers and television, that we are the preeminent nation. This has been true in many respects, becoming an American mindset. Does this past truth guarantee that we have nothing to contribute or do to maintain it? History will record our contributions. Are we to be recorded as the weakest link in the chain?

*** For a complete understanding of the "great depression that nearly happened" (my quote) see, "Bailout" by Neil Borofsky – every American should read it!
**** "Ideas That Matter" by A.C. Grayling

Reality is beginning to paint a slightly different picture from that mindset. During the middle of the 20th century we developed the largest and wealthiest "middle-class" the world has ever known. As a consequence of the G.I. Bill, after World War II, millions of returning veterans secured a college education which produced a strong, productive workforce and a robust economy. This created a nation of consumers and the American dream was actualized for millions. The continuance of consumer demand relies entirely on a well-paid workforce throughout the nation – a maldistribution of wealth always spells doom to the national economy.

During that time we embarked upon an impressive development of our national infrastructure which invigorated the economy and changed America. Con- currently our educational system was rated the world's best. Was that the Golden age of our democracy? Taking lessons from the 1950s and 1960s let us resolve to do better, redeem and enhance our republic and put our best years ahead of us.

In the mid 20th century the average difference in income between the lowest paid full-time wage earner and the highest-paid executive of the same company was approximately $1-$35. Today that ratio is about $1-$343. In that earlier time we developed dominant economic and educational systems. As a society we pursued life as if things would never change, as if good times could be taken for granted.

As a result societal values changed and a hedonistic wave crossed the country. A new mindset developed and we transformed from a "quality-of-life" basis to a "material wealth" concept and it became a dominant feature of our culture as we entered the 21st century. Money, as a master of our culture and our value system, will dominate our social and political actions and therefore our lives. Under these conditions society has always divided into classes defined by the haves and the have-nots. The result predicts that our republic will slowly recede to become only a placebo to appease that portion of the public who have failed to make it to the "upper-class". These circumstances are not the "preeminence" we seek.

Our innate characteristics are well known. The good side of our nature has produced great things. But, these characteristics also include greed which, held in bounds, may be beneficial both personally and to society. "Educated greed" can translate into innovations and accomplishment for betterment or it can evolve into avarice where there are no bounds and society suffers. Seemingly there will always be those for whom there is never enough and these excesses will always have the same effect as any other antisocial behavior. A society whose values are well-placed will protect itself from such excesses. Societal well-being should always be held above individual interests when they cannot be reconciled.

In the last part of the 20th and early 21st century our "middle-class" dwindled significantly; global corporations began to predominate economically while our educational system was being surpassed by virtually every industrialized nation. Concurrently a technological revolution was occurring and having far more social effects than our body politic has recognized. Ideas and opinions are circulated worldwide and people consider new views daily on just about everything, for good or for bad. It has vast significance for our society and our governance including our foreign relations. The fact must be accepted that people are all the same, they generally think and want the same things. Never be deluded to think that we are fundamentally different due to differences of culture and ethnicity.

The consequences of the web are only beginning to be recognized for its influence on hundreds of millions of users around the world. It provides the potential for people of the world to come together provided we can develop unified messages directed toward goodwill; otherwise it can have an opposite effect. Effects are seen in every nation. The web should be used to educate people everywhere about democracy. It is a venue for typical citizens to utilize a common message of friendship as well as highlighting democracy. Public leaders should fashion scripts portraying democracy and distribute them to those interested in becoming a goodwill ambassador. World peace could hinge on people to people exchanges.

Concurrently the rest of the world has been changing also. Globalized economies in the form of scores of international corporations are changing many nations –China, Russia, the near east Emirates, India,

Indonesia and parts of South America and Africa. These nations practice "state capitalism" whereby national governments own and direct enormous surplus funds as a factor of national policy and an agent in foreign relations. Their investments are noticeable factors in the corporate policies of several transnational corporations. In one year, 2012, China's capital funds invested nearly $8 billion in corporations doing business in the United States. Their avowed aim is profit and they pursue this goal with "friendly and cooperative" governments and they have the financial strength and know-how through lobbying firms, to win friends and influence legislators, as well as a few governmental regulators.*****

Speculation abounds on what this portends for the United States. But a few things are obvious – China has a population six times that of the US and their exports far exceed their imports which amasses great sums of money in their state funds; India has three times as many people as the US and they too are progressing rapidly, especially in technology; both Russia and Indonesia are almost as large as the United States and the latter is growing rapidly. All the others combined are about equal to the United States. There are many other countries pursuing this same strategy including Saudi Arabia which is among the wealthiest, Kuwait, Brazil, Chile, South Korea and oil rich Abu Dhabi which may be the wealthiest of all. Note that only two or three of these nations could be described as republics.

Many of these state capitalist funds may, indeed, have profit as their principle motive. However when one considers our national interests it would be prudent to take necessary steps for protection. Should all corporations doing business in the United States be required to assert their allegiance to the Constitution of the United States as a required part of their incorporation? In addition, should all of their activities, particularly in the fields of cybernetics and electronics, be closely monitored?

***** For a comprehensive picture of state capitalism see "The End of the Free Market" by Ian Bremmer

The vast wealth of these nations based upon the worldwide demand for their natural resources and/or their cheap labor, allows them to accumulate staggering amounts of money. These funds are used to buy into successful corporations doing business in several countries. With such a vested interest the ruling national elite of these countries has little tolerance for democratic rule and the focus of their business interests rests solely on profits and control. Dedication to such principles as human rights and democratic rule play no part in their operations which would be diametrically opposed to their interests. This, then, is an emerging threat to social and economic justice and equality under law to which we should pay close attention.

Is the intrusion of such vast wealth into political campaigns with no public knowledge of where the money comes from a dire threat to public control over government? Today many, if not most of our representatives are more dependent upon this type of financial assistance than on the public they presumably represent. Is it realistic to conjecture whether giant international corporations are the source of most of this money? Are our arrangements for representative government with no effective controls on campaign financing capable of resisting this new world picture? What is the best defense against this insidious invasion which utilizes our free society to work against us? The answers lie in a better organizational structure to secure true representation where money is not an issue, which will provide the best defense. Vested interests will be opposed but we have the means if we have the will to erect this defense.

Terrorists also pose a threat but they are much more visible and could never accomplish the fundamental disruption or secure the legal advantages with which we are now faced– that of purchasing favors and special privileges through both administrative and Congressional venues. Terrorists can be controlled and defeated militarily but insidious intrusions into our economy and our political governance cannot be controlled or defeated militarily – only we can do that!

Constituent features in a republic's arsenal which must be in working order, include first of all, an informed and educated electorate. This requires that there be a legal right to universal public education. It was

IS THE UNITED STATES WORTH SAVING?

James Madison who said "knowledge will forever govern ignorance and a people who mean to be their own governors, must arm themselves with the power knowledge gives." Second, there must be constitutional safeguards to ensure voting rights for all citizens, managed by bipartisan electoral boards and by judicial means. Third, we must end the anti-democratic practice of gerrymandering and provide methods to select competent congressman by requiring a true vetting process. Fourth, laws which provide special privileges, rights or economic advantage without a clear, demonstrable public necessity must be constitutionally forbidden.

Only when we have representatives who are fully accountable to the public can we guarantee and perform these assignments. Before it is too late we must critically examine what kind of nation and society we have become and what we want and should be. By doing so we will realize that we must use our nation's intelligence to help point us in the right direction.

We must reform our system of representation to ensure that public voices are heard. A reformed system of representation will examine and correct those circumstances which permit laws and regulations that provide special exemptions or privilege whether it be in taxation, product safety or in environmental safeguards. Only then can a free competitive enterprise system become feasible.

There must be protections for members of Congress and their staffs to ensure that they are not targets for special interests which seek favorable considerations. An open public record should be required for all contacts with public representatives. If they are performing public business it is reasonable to allow the public some knowledge of the process and participants. If our constitutional guarantee of equal protection of the laws can be made meaningful then society will be the recipient of its benefits. In the development of national policies, the public should have access to all the names of all parties who have participated in any way with its formulation. An exception should be allowed only on matters of national security. Adequate safeguards should be in place to ensure that any such exemption meets all of the tests for national security.

Can there be serious doubt whether arrangements formulated in the 18th century, which established representative government, meets 21st century reality? If our Constitutional framers were drafting the documents facing today's realities, how many changes would they make? Could they have known that there would be some 25,000 lobbyists registered in Washington DC before the end of the first decade of the 21st century? This is a number close to the total population of the largest city in the 13 colonies in 1776! It is a number which blossomed from some 5000 registered lobbyists in the mid-1990s. Could they have known that some congress members would take an oath to perform one of their duties in accordance with the wishes of a private party? There is absolutely no realistic comparison between the original 13 states, their culture, society or economy and our modern-day America.

The very definition of a republic is based on the requirement for representation of the people. Could our forefathers have known about such a staggering influence of lobbyists, the introduction of hundreds of millions of dollars into political campaigns or even gerrymandered congressional districts? It only required Elbridge Gerry some 20 years to figure out how to always be reelected! He managed to reconfigure his district to bring in all the areas containing his supporters. Mr. Gerry was very well known, having been a member of the constitutional convention. The case was heard before the Supreme Court in the early 1800s where his district was described as looking like a salamander. The court, however, upheld the redistricting only requiring that a district be contiguous. The court did say that the district looked more like a gerrymander! With that ruling representative government in America began its descent from democracy. Does common sense tell us that we are a captive audience?

The 17th amendment of the Constitution in 1913 provided for the direct election of senators by the people. Senators no longer represent states; they represent the people of the state. But state populations are far from equal and we now have the paradox where a few states have more senators representing the people of their state than they have representatives in the House. Recall that the original Constitution established the Senate to represent states, not the people. A century and a quarter later we got around to establishing a more democratic republic by deciding to represent people in the Senate. This was an acknowledgment that we were meant to be a republic, not a Balkanized Confederacy of helpless states.

There are now six states with fewer than 1 million people. There is one state, California, with a population roughly equal to 20 of the smallest states. From the standpoint of representation it takes 58 citizens in California to receive the same representation as one person does in Wyoming, North Dakota, South Dakota, Alaska or Vermont. Texas is in a somewhat similar situation having roughly a population equal to 15 of our smallest states.

These two states, California and Texas, have approximately 56,000,000 people which constitute more than 1/6 of the nation's population. Think of it, one out of every six Americans live in either California or Texas. Even more astounding is the fact that nearly one out of every three Americans lives in four states, California, Texas, New York or Florida. It would take 25 of our smallest states, population wise, to be their equal. Those 25 states constitute one half the membership of the entire United States Senate. California and Texas constitute 1/25th.

Four of our states, California, Texas, New York and Florida have 92 million people, nearly one third of the nation's population. On a population basis they should have 31 senators not eight. This imbalance could be corrected by allotting value to senatorial votes on the basis of state population. Should the Constitution be revised to better represent American citizens or shall it represent tracts of land whose boundaries are fictitious lines? If the latter choice is true then how can we call our government a republic? How long shall we abide by an arrangement which has no relevance to today's reality? This situation clearly illustrates how prolonged growth and changing conditions result in highly significant effects and seemingly have no relevance to our founding values and purpose.

These facts illustrate also how growth and expansion have developed a very disproportionate representation which was not intended or envisioned in 1789. With such a glaring example it is only pretense to say that we believe in a republic that represents its citizens. Our government was not designed to be Balkanized as if Americans in each section of the country were to have a different and distinct culture. We are all Americans, accept and believe in the same Constitution and want to live our lives in a republic. Is it logical to continue as if these conditions do not matter, that representation of citizens is inconsequential?

For many years since the early 1900s following World War I, we have been a nation on the move. It is common today for a citizen to have lived in two, three or even more states during their lifetime. Numerous people work their entire lives in one state and retire in another. A large number of people work in virtually all states and many are transferred by their companies every four or five years. The search for opportunity, better living conditions, business requirements, and a better place to retire, as well as for other reasons, has caused our citizenry to ignore state lines.

Since the beginning of the 20th century, as a nation, we are one and we might safely speculate that at least 99% of Americans would choose national patriotism above that of their state. Are we fair-minded and realistic enough to recognize these facts legally and rise above the myth of state sovereignty? With perhaps only three or four exceptions no state could exist as an independent government and they would find their existence precarious. All states depend on and are enriched by our union.

Before some readers might feel a bit dismayed by this last statement be assured that it is not intended to suggest that we expunge the idea of federalism. Rather it is to recognize 21st century reality in two ways: first, improve and revitalize our republican principles by more favorably representing people rather than plots of ground, and secondly, focusing on present-day problems of providing and protecting fundamental rights as well as the difficulties attendant to dealing with international affairs. This is where the rise of state capitalism can play an ever greater influence on local and state governments, which are less equipped and less likely to be aware of the potential consequences in their dealings with these entities. This is where provincial interests, attitudes and policies have the potential to endanger the entire nation. We should not allow foreign entities to invade us state-by-state!

Aspects of federalism still have a principal role to play in a free governmental system. Starting with home rule for cities and the right of states to form their own governments, states would be protected still by our federal Constitution. Federalism also has the advantage to allow for experimentation and innovation in public practices. Numerous worthwhile plans and programs, as well as administrative arrangements, have been developed under this unique organization of governmental powers. Unitary governments fail to realize this advantage. These local freedoms, sovereignty if you will, must remain as they provide another guard, along with our national Constitution, against unlimited national power.

In the annals of history few governmental forms have lasted much longer than the United States. This raises worrying questions as to whether or not our experience in democracy is in decline as result of our failures to remedy the flaws which time and experience has shown to exist. A cause of many failures has been due to a reluctance to change and by clinging to ideas, methods and/or arrangements long after their usefulness has expired. Can the lessons of history, our intelligence and belief in democracy triumph over parochial biases?

Meaningful topics of this type require informed debate. Perhaps the most difficult part in arriving at answers to such questions is to do so with true objectivity. We all carry with us ideas and concepts we have learned, felt right about, and have pursued for years as perhaps the most dependable answers regarding all the things with which we have had to deal. But hopefully we have not come to such a complacent and comfortable milestone as to expect nature's bounty without effort, without sacrifice and without knowing and understanding that the gift of liberty is neither automatic nor is it free – too many lives and too much human misery has been expended for us not to be willing to consider new ideas to preserve the liberties for which so many have sacrificed.

Is the United States the last best hope for democracy in the world? Ponder what our founding fathers achieved against all odds in bringing forth the new nation which we have had the privilege to inherit, to prosper and to enjoy. Ask yourself what you are willing to do with it and whether we owe anything to those who gave their lives to preserve it. Do we have an obligation to posterity? Given the cracks in the armor of our republic, is it logical to ask how long it can last if we continue as we have and do nothing to make fundamental changes? We are that link in the chain of humanity which is destined to leave our contribution, good or bad, to the cause of free government on earth. This is truly a pivotal time in our nation's history – the fate of true republican government is at stake.

Considering our present condition regarding public representation, our economic practices and social mores, many intriguing and provocative questions arise which deserve serious consideration if not complete answers. Many of these will elicit some biases and preconceived ideas or they may take us back a step to recall what a miraculous thing our forefathers conceived of so many years ago. Over the past two centuries one could compare us to any other society in the world and there would be very few who would consider taking permanent residence elsewhere. Today, however, could we hazard the same dare? In many fields of endeavor we have begun to lag behind to the detriment of many millions of our citizens. Our educational system and our aging infrastructure lags behind and both impose dangers to public welfare as well as a hindrance to commerce and economic development.

The zeal and spirit of liberty which brought this republic into being has not been manifested regularly during the past few decades. We seem to have been coasting along on board our inheritance without continuing to add real fundamental and substantive corrections to our governance. The basis of all of this rests and depends on our social values, altruism and our dedication to democracy. If the present is not a good time to administer aid to an impaired republic, when will there be a better time? Will there ever be a better time?

Our nation is one of great diversity and there is no single description to adequately describe our value system. There are aspects of many cultures to be found in various sections of today's America. America has long been called a melting pot of cultures and ethnicity. It has resulted in a great variety emblematic of the world's people. Our focus must stress the things which all cultures strive for – liberty, safety, justice and opportunity – amalgamated through our common humanity and solidified through universal public education.

Symbolically our experiment in republican government places us in a time capsule test tube to determine whether Montesquieu or Madison was correct. So far Madison would appear to have been correct but the final verdict has not been rendered. It is history and time which points its finger at us for the final answer.

Our diversity may be our salvation. Over time the more successful and rewarding habits, customs, activities and general lifestyles are more likely to prevail. Every culture has its strengths and its weaknesses. Passing fads are products of virtually every generation and they remain that, a passing fad. Little has changed over the millenniums of known history which tells us that a child born today is essentially no different than one born 4,000 to 5,000 years ago. We read of the anguish of ancient Greek parents bemoaning the impudence of their children. So we see that people are essentially the same and they will respond to the same stimuli. It is up to us to provide appropriate stimuli to build and protect the kind of society we wish to live in. It is through good parenting, a comprehensive educational system and public insistence on placing meaningful and ethical characteristics and attributes into our social values that, as a society, we will evolve a more common culture which will allow us to improve and progress as a people and as a nation.

The histories of past civilizations can teach us many things. Their experience represents what people are likely to do. They expose the fact that internal intrigues to gain power, public acclaim, fortune, along with the attendant loss of any regard for founding values, leads to a disengagement between the duty to serve public welfare and that of the personal ambitions of those who would lead. These factors have been commonly noticed to be the death knell of many governments. It is for we the people to understand and insist that our founding values are first and foremost in our governance – if we don't, who will?

It is only true democratic governance which can offer a realistic chance to actualize the common aspirations of all people. To those whom much has been given, much should be expected – does this parable apply to us? We have been given a valid prescription for a type of government, documented in the Declaration of Independence and the constitution's preamble, which is able to provide what all people want.

If the United States is worth saving let us improve it for the 21st century and beyond. We are the generation which must answer – failure must not happen on our watch! So, why is the United States worth saving? Because it is the last hope for people of the world to witness the blessings of liberty! Let William H. Seward, Secretary of State under President Lincoln give his answer after a long tour of Europe caused him to realize "the fearful responsibility of the American people to the nations of the whole earth, to carry successfully through the experiment which…..is to prove that men are capable of self-government. If some misguided American should imagine that a northern or a southern, an eastern or a western confederacy, or the independence of [one state] would still be enough to accomplish this great purpose of providing the capability of man for self-government, he would find that it is only as a whole, one great, flourishing, united, happy people, that the United States command respect abroad. If the union were dissolved, its separate states would sink below the level of the South American states."[******]

[******] "Seward" by Walter Stahr

(Plato) "He sees a social vision too, and dreams of a society in which there shall be no corruption, no poverty, no tyranny, and no war. He is appalled at the bitterness and political faction in Athens, 'strife and enmity and hatred and suspicion forever recurring.' like a blueblood, he despises the plutocratic oligarchy, 'the man of business…. pretending never so much as to see those whom they have already ruined, inserting their sting – that is, their money – into anybody else who is not on his guard against them, and recovering the principal sum many times over: this is the way in which they make drones and paupers to abound in the state.'"

**The Story of Civilization:
Part II, The Life of Greece, Will Durant**

CHAPTER 2

To Form a More Perfect Union

> Why ratify the Constitution? The great principle of self-preservation; to the transcendent law of nature and of nature's God, which declares that the safety and happiness of society are the objects at which all political institution aims and to which all such institutions must be sacrificed.
> The Federalist papers, X L III

Our constitutional framers dedicated their work to one central cause – to form a more perfect union – the heart and soul of our founding values. This short phrase addresses the direction, the purpose, for our nation. It proclaims a goal that everyone should want to achieve, not individually, but as a society – if the better side of our humanity can prevail. From the earliest of historical times people have striven to find ways to be free and to live together – two seemingly disparate goals but two indispensable requirements for safety and survival.

For thousands of years the world has been adding more and more people. From the earliest known times there has been the requirement for some sort of social organization. Having a gregarious nature people banded together for many reasons, safety being most likely a prominent reason together with advantages to provide other essentials of life. Safety is the foremost ingredient of survival. It is foremost also among the functions of our republic.

The early civilizations of Egypt and Mesopotamia were governed by cult, myth and idols. As populations grew, inhabiting Africa, Asia and Europe, kingdoms formed around theological concepts, eventually giving rise to rule by the "divine right of Kings". Monarchies were born. The general public became serfs or slaves and a class system evolved. In ancient Greece, Plato conceived of a republic but even his "Republic" in the fourth century B.C. restricted citizenship to one class. Nevertheless, it was a beginning. In Rome, a few centuries later, other attempts were made to form a republic but their attempts, for the most part, were relatively short-lived and relied on a cadre of a few men. At no time, however, did people come together purposely to form a republic with written rules and organizational plans to implement and preserve it – that is, until 1788.

It is inconceivable how anyone would object to the notion of forming a more perfect union. This is an ideal about which many have espoused over the ages. From Plato's Republic, Sir Thomas More's "Utopia" in 1516 to Samuel Butler's "Erewhon" in 1872, mankind has dreamed of a near paradise on earth. These are indicative of human aspirations for a more perfect union. They symbolize the eternal hope of mankind for utopia on earth, to find that lost Eden, or to reach the "promised land" provided the better nature of mankind could prevail and by utilizing our intelligence to predominate over the happenstance of daily practice.

So in addition to questions about how this more perfect union can be formulated and put into practice there remains the lingering problem about the nature of humankind and whether the good side or the bad side will prevail. It is our social mores which reveal what we really are as a people and they will predict the kind of governance which will eventually gain ascendancy. There must be a concerted public effort to set forth better alternatives for a safer, more ethical and altruistic social order to provide a society for all to enjoy.

Since the mind of man has been thinking about a more perfect union, writing about it, is it actually in the realm of possibility? Unlike the earlier utopias our constitutional framers were well aware that what they had drafted was not a perfect document –they considered it an experiment! As an experiment we have found it necessary and desirable to amend the original Constitution 27 times. We must now rely upon citizen desire and determination to be directed toward establishing improved governance. Are today's citizens now capable of advancing and instituting new amendments to proceed toward a more perfect union?

The path to a more perfect union could take numerous forms provided the main ingredients are present and preserved. Personal liberty, equal justice and true public representation are prerequisites for a republic. Parenting, early life experiences, personal characteristics and education are among the vital factors leading to various concepts regarding the pursuit of happiness in a more perfect union. General agreement can be found regarding the value of personal liberty, equal protection under law, opportunity, health and safety as required factors to pursue the "American dream". What would life be like without any of these?

A prerequisite for a more perfect union requires that no one is left out – it must be totally inclusive. Realistically it must be recognized that everyone will not reap the same material rewards even in a free society and a competitive economy. Notwithstanding reality, no worthwhile social culture can ignore any human being and some provision will always be required to address the most unfortunate among us. No human being is without dignity and no one should be reduced to begging – medieval cultural features have no place in a true republic.

Our early colonies were largely populated by those who fled from religious persecution and from caste based societies where opportunity was restricted and hope for improvement was virtually nonexistent. Our forefathers wanted no part of this type of society or with a monarchy based on the divine right of Kings. It required eight grueling years of war to gain the rights which are preserved in our Constitution and given freely to us. We have been reaping what was given to us with little concern for what will be left to posterity. The constitutional framers thought of us; can we say the same thing about future generations?

IS THE UNITED STATES WORTH SAVING?

Throughout the ages mankind has managed to corrupt virtually everything from family life, sectarian organizations, corporations, government and even religion. Therefore we must endeavor to structure our government to provide strict safeguards and protections which experience has shown to be necessary. This is the constitutional way to guard against human weaknesses, reduce temptation and minimize their adverse effects on society. This is the way a democracy survives – no revolutions and no bloody uprisings – through deliberated decisions of educated, fair-minded citizens considering only the public interest.

Constitutionally we should require ethical conduct in governmental service. The Constitution should define ethical conduct by specifying its purpose, its areas of application, its consequences for violation and a requirement that Congress must pass a comprehensive ethics law fulfilling these requirements before they can receive any compensation. Such law should prohibit the acceptance of any type of financial aid, gift, or thing of value or personal favors. Our objective should be to create a secure climate for true public service and to protect those who desire to serve. To change the culture of Washington DC is essential for the formation of a more perfect union. President Abraham Lincoln told us "it is as much the duty of government to render prompt justice against itself, in favor of citizens, as it is to administer the same between individuals."

Fundamental to democracy is how the relationship between those who govern and the governed is formulated and accomplished in practice. How this relationship is effectuated and maintained constitutes the essence of democracy. Who the new union should serve and who was included seems to have been reasonably answered. First we note that one of the six founding criteria of the Constitution is to promote the general welfare. The word "general" seems to provide little room for exceptions. However, it required two centuries and seven amendments to ensure the fact for legal purposes. These seven amendments have attempted to remove all doubt.

- The 13th amendment, 1865, prohibits slavery and involuntary servitude except as punishment for crimes for which there has been a conviction.

- The 14th amendment, 1868, provides that everyone born or naturalized in the United States and subject to its jurisdiction is a citizen of the United States and the state where they reside. No state can make or enforce any law to abridge privileges or immunities of US citizens or deprive any person of life, liberty or property without due process of law or deny them the equal protection of laws.

- The 15th amendment, 1870, provides the right to vote which cannot be abridged by the United States or any state on account of race, color or previous condition of servitude.

- The 19th amendment, 1920, provides that a citizen's right to vote cannot be denied or abridged based on gender.

- The 23rd amendment, 1961, provides citizens of the District of Columbia the right to vote for president and that the district shall have the same number of presidential electors as if it were a state, provided that they are not to have more electoral votes than the least populous state.

- The 24th amendment, 1964, provides to all citizens the right to vote for president and vice president, senators and representatives in Congress and such right cannot be denied for failure to pay any poll tax or other tax.

- The 26th amendment, 1971, provides the right to vote to citizens who are 18 years of age or older and such right cannot be denied or abridged by the United States or any state on account of age.

In spite of this there remain efforts in a number of states to limit and restrict voting rights to American citizens. It becomes obvious that unprincipled party zeal overshadows any understanding or belief in democracy. To protect every citizen's absolute right to vote is a niche apparently left vacant in our constitutional guarantees – a vital democratic principle and necessity for a republic. This problem needs to be addressed by establishing national standards for the conduct of elections including placing their administration in a bipartisan arrangement. Is there any true American who will publicly oppose such a right? No state should be given the opportunity to purposefully design or structure the fundamental right of voting to affect election results, especially federal representatives who have an impact on the entire nation.

Unfortunately we have seen many attempts to rig elections and those attempts have become more sophisticated in recent years. A complete list would be too long to enumerate. A sampling of the devices, procedures and maneuvers include faulty voting machines, including those with no verifiable record, confusing arrangements of ballots, limiting the time for voting, restricting the number and locations of polling places, covert intimidation, misleading public advertising regarding election times and hours and the restriction of methods and means for identification of voters. Do any of these practices enhance our endeavors to form a more perfect union? What kind of citizenship promotes such practices? Restricting any valid right to vote is tantamount to disallowing freedom of speech – voting is how the public speaks!**

Too many political campaigns have become a disgrace to the ideal of democracy. The lack of legal controls, a lack of dependable public exposure to deceptive claims and outright misrepresentation of fact has left the voting public dismayed and confused. We see public officials who openly attempt (and often accomplish) to alter or disallow voting rights. We see measures that were once adopted to give the public a voice in government policy, such as the initiative and referendum, turn to political chicanery where special interests use them to place self serving measures on the ballot and rely on millions of dollars of advertising to lure the voting public to their will. A thorough, 21st-century overhaul is needed!

---

*   For a comprehensive treatise on voting see "The Voting Wars" by Richard L. Hasen

The infamous Nazi propagandist, Joseph Goebbels, stated that he had forged the Nazi regime, Hitler's Reich, with his propaganda. The big lie, he said, can be sold if repeated long enough. It destroyed the Weimar Republic in Germany! Are we immune? We are now seeing the same strategy being used on us. We must comprehend the fact that all human institutions, including our society, never remain still. They are in a constant state of evolution. It is for this reason that we must intelligently develop a path for social and political improvement or else they will degrade. In practical politics it seems axiomatic to gain personal advantage by whatever means are available – ethical, accurate or not!

Any attempt to confuse the voting public is typical of totalitarian methods used to gain and hold power by restricting fundamental rights of citizens to choose their representatives or to see and understand clearly real national issues. Many tactics are used: misrepresentation of facts, finding a hate target, scare tactics, cleverly worded proposals and advertisements meant to achieve an opposite result from what they at first appear to be, etc. All such tactics are unacceptable in a republic for they undermine fundamental citizen obligations and responsibilities to have their voices heard. The authorization to put in practice such schemes is, in effect, treasonable. They are overt attacks against the foundation of our republic and should be addressed as such by legal restrictions.

How we select the president becomes a vital element in whether our government can be classified as a republic. Consider the fact that the president is the only office that is selected by and responsible to all of the people. Our nation must place great reliance on the personal character, qualifications, leadership and his/her philosophy for the country. The direction of the nation and welfare of the American people rests heavily on the shoulders of the person in this office. The respect and confidence for the person in this office is not improved when elected by less than a majority of the public or when the election results have been manipulated by limiting voting possibilities of citizens.

The days of the Electoral College has long since served its usefulness and value. It was never in harmony with democratic principles and actually reflected our constitutional framers fears of the "common man". The enormous disparity in the population of the states, the common lifestyle of citizens to move from state to state, indicates that representation of people, not legal boundaries, should prevail in the election of the nation's only representative. The Constitution should be amended to provide for the direct election of the president and vice president.

The many questions to be asked on how this more perfect union is to be formulated and put into practice will evoke many and varied conceptual ideas. The subject is prone also to bring forth one's ideology, biases, parochial interests or allegiance as well as one's political party devotion. Hopefully, if not realistically, we may be spared most of these barriers if we are able to restrict ourselves to building on what we have inherited and realizing that what we do or fail to do in our time, whether it is good or bad, will have repercussions for generations to come. Let us focus only on what enhances and ensures a true republic.

During our lifetime could we ever receive greater comfort and compensation than to improve and pass along a greater republic to the generations which follow us? What we do will define us, not what we have said. Let us use a fundamental test for proposals, requiring that all of them must accept and reinforce liberty, equality and the dignity and self-worth of every human being – no exclusions.

Most people believe that our original concept of a republic was a gigantic leap compared to the earlier precepts of ancient Greece and Rome. Indeed it was remarkable and impressive but, in reality, there were several parallels between the original Constitution as submitted and some concepts of those early kingdoms. It has taken a Bill of Rights, a civil war, nine more amendments and nearly 2 centuries to qualify for that gargantuan leap to distinction. We remain a work in progress regarding both governmental form and public involvement.

A republic is a government where power is vested in the people and is exercised by the ones chosen to represent them. How that relationship is conducted becomes essential. To effectuate this definition consists of performing free and honest elections, choosing competent representatives who are responsible to those who elect them while requiring political campaigns to be conducted on real issues. If any citizen should wonder why Congress fails to act on many common sense issues, from fair taxation, subsidies and exemptions to those who don't need it, to reasonable gun control or to green energy, just examine where your representative gets his or her campaign financing. As things stand today, how would you answer the question: who exerts the most influence on "our" representatives – big financial contributors or the voters?

It is imperative that we devise better ways to actualize in practice the tenets of democracy. We must question whether our vote today receives representation. We have to question whether our voting districts are manipulated to ensure the election of a particular party's candidate. The only legal requirement is that the district be "contiguous", a relic based on an early 19th century Supreme Court ruling. With that perfunctory requirement districts spread over many miles and take shapes which cannot be described. The greatest common interest in such districts is political party registration. Considering this, we find that more than 80% of members of the House of Representatives run in districts specifically designed to heavily favor their party. In a recent election more than 80% of incumbents won reelection, in spite of the fact that public opinion polls reflected a public approval rating of about 12%! To minimize this practice, voter registration should show either no party affiliation or party registration should not be open for public exposure. Preferably the members of Congress should be elected statewide, or at the very least, from equalized congressional districts arranged by some kind of nonpartisan procedure.

A stronger logical reason for statewide election of congressional members, considering they hold a national office, is to avoid the ability of one single group to hold the entire nation hostage. A few congressmen representing politically safe, gerrymandered districts are now able to block the entire governmental system. This can be done even when their state has elected senators, or a governor, or the president who represent a different political party and elected to achieve programs which the people of the nation or state have endorsed! We have witnessed this very situation which puts our entire nation in perilous circumstances. This is exactly what President George Washington warned could happen! Shouldn't we learn from his sage advice and benefit from experience?

Another peril which must be averted is threats against congressional members. These are not physical threats but financial threats which are blatant attempts to direct national policy for some individual preference, profit and benefit. The threat of withholding financial campaign aid, which would be directed toward some future opponent, is the leverage they possess. Every observer of this scene is aware that many members of Congress become a pawn to special interests rather than being allowed to serve their nation.

Democratic government requires fair elections to represent public opinion which requires a valid choice between or among contesting viewpoints. At issue is how members of Congress are chosen and whether gerrymandered districts meet that test of a fair election process. There is no honest way to equate gerrymandering as being compatible with democracy, the fundamental aim and purpose of our Constitution. This outdated scheme, freely utilized by both political parties, has emerged into a nationwide practice. Simply by redesigning districts through the use of demographic and political party registrations, the party in power can gain additional representation in Congress with no change in the total population and thereby affect national policies. This illustration reflects how public permissiveness allows alterations in the list of fundamental democratic principles, to result in the loss of citizens' rights.

When the public does not respond to political duplicity there will be a vacuum in the democratic structure creating room for those who can and will use government for their personal reasons – there are some 25,000 lobbyists in Washington DC who are busy doing just that! So, who gets represented?

Realistically then, most current congress members, certain political leaders and financial contributors decide who the representative will be. This being the case to whom does the representative owe their allegiance? This becomes more apparent when a representative is moved from one place of residence to another after electoral districts are realigned. If we are bound to elect congress members from districts, a safeguard could be to require that any candidate seeking to represent a district should be required to live in that district for not less than one year. At least this could develop some knowledge and understanding on the part of the candidates with the needs and circumstances of the district they presume to represent – and perhaps, allow the people to know "their" chosen candidate.

Gerrymandered districts also ignore city and county boundaries where we often find communities of common interests, problems and needs. Our courts, as well as state laws, have failed to correct this obvious political scheme. It is heartbreaking to see, in retrospect, how some Supreme Court rulings have debased our republican form of government. Since the entire Constitution is designed for the express purpose of forming a republic therefore, the constitutionality of all laws should be in harmony with this objective and intent. When a law or practice violates the very definition and purpose of a republic it has to be inimical to the Constitution.

A better safeguard worthy of consideration would be to require all congressional representatives to run at large. Each political party could be accorded the number of seats in comparison with their percentage of the total vote – the prevailing party being given the advantage of any fraction remaining. This type of procedure would have many advantages recognizing the fact that everyone in the state has many common interests. It should be kept in mind that Congress deals specifically in national interests and not state issues. The Constitution specifies only that representatives are to be chosen based upon the state's total population. When the Constitution was written there were no political parties. Why then should the rules of a republic be designed to cater to a political party's interests rather than to maximize public controls and preference? Isn't securing public representation our real objective? Members of Congress need to be free of parochial restraints.

It is not uncommon for a representative to remain in office for 20 years or more and although facing election every two years many

Congressman rarely have to campaign accept to make a few public appearances. In most of these districts the opposition party rarely enters a credible candidate except for the purpose of causing the incumbent election expense. How does this situation equate to our definition of a republic? Recognizing that members of Congress are federal officials there should be more specific constitutional guidelines governing their selection, particularly with reference to qualifications and residency.

If we must be saddled with congressional districts, for the sake of democracy the configuration of Congressional districts should be placed in the hands of a bipartisan citizen's commission. A recent example of this approach is seen in the state of California where, by a vote of the people, such a commission was established. Legal criteria were established with its prime motive to equalize political party registrations in each district. Obviously it is impossible to redistrict an entire state, especially one as large as California, with perfectly balanced districts. This was made doubly difficult by other legal criteria such as recognition of ethnicity. Even this criterion is not totally compatible with the tenets of a true democracy. But until we become a people where we realize and accept the fact that we are all alike and that laws and regulations should not be allowed which favor or become detrimental to anyone on the basis of ethnicity then, until such time, such criteria will need to stand. However, practical difficulties to the contrary, the results of the California experience appear to be superior in comparison to politically gerrymandered districts.

The results of extreme party partisanship has served to confirm the apprehension of our first president, the father of our country, that it would lead to bitter divisiveness which in turn could set the stage for an ungovernable country. From the earliest days we can witness the prophetic truth of President Washington's warning. The father of our country in his farewell address also said "however, political parties, may now and then answer popular ends, they are likely in the course of time and things, to become potent engines, by which cunning, ambitious, and unprincipled men will be enabled to subvert the power of the people and to usurp for themselves the reins of government, destroying afterwards the very engines which have lifted them to unjust dominion."

This problem was even recognized in ancient Greece when Aristotle voiced a similar warning of a tendency for people to organize into narrow self interest groups without regard for the greater good of society. The bitterness engendered by political campaigns has been a common occurrence throughout our history. The fact of its commonality however should not be dismissed as not having serious consequences to our national unity. Dating back to the mid-1820s we find that "One of the Auburn (N. Y.) papers 'lamented, politics are the only species of warfare that admits of no cessation of hostilities. There is reason to fear that the frequency of elections in this country, connected with the bitterness and asperity with which they are conducted, have produced a belligerent state of feeling.' "**

Until a better method is devised to elect our representatives we must accept reality, and in spite of the contradictions to democracy, we seem destined to practice representative government through political parties. Facing that reality would it not seem best to require all political activity to be as compatible with republican principles as possible? In such a case it would be appropriate to institutionalize this approach and provide guidelines and requirements in our Constitution to prohibit demagogic campaign practices. Political campaigns would be conducted via legal guidelines and political parties would no longer be in that "extra-legal world," they would become a legally valid and responsible part of the governmental system.

Provisions could be made to require each party to publish annually a complete platform of the party's beliefs and objectives, including their program to address public issues, needs and problems. An added proviso should be that all parties avow allegiance to the Constitution. This would provide a strong incentive for candidates to either declare their allegiance to those beliefs and objectives or to publicly indicate their exceptions to them. The citizens would be given a clear choice on how to cast their ballot. Would it even be possible to devise some guidelines to restrict politicking during Congressional sessions – a fanciful thought

---

** "Seward" by Walter Stahr

but wouldn't it be great to have a Congress where members would have to work on public business only?

Of fundamental importance is the method and procedure for selection of candidates – a most vital component in the determination of who will best represent us. Today party leaders, financial backers , make that choice. Does this procedure correspond to democracy? Can we achieve something closer to the ideal of "having the office choosing the candidate rather than the candidate choosing the office?" Why should we not require every candidate to file a complete application – a resume of their qualifications and their personal beliefs, ideas etc? Is it not an anomaly to require a complete application and background check in order to hire anyone for a job, even jobs of relatively lesser importance, and ignore checking qualifications for an office which affects our lives and our nation? Today the voter is left with whoever a few party leaders present to them.

These approaches would be a strong incentive for political parties to endeavor to put forward competent candidates and to address real public issues – their needs and requirements. It would also allow the voter to better determine where their support should be directed. This approach would tend to minimize what seems to be a human trait to have a lifelong allegiance to one party regardless of their own personal best interests or how that party has changed positions over time. The voter would be given a much better chance to cast an intelligent vote. In any case the interests of our republic would be better served and governmental decisions would more closely reflect public conditions and opinion.

All of this would help to counteract a growing and dangerous trend of voter disenchantment for politics. Citizen apathy and lack of knowledge regarding public issues constitutes a chilling and horrifying prospect for the continuance of democracy. Voter turnout, across the nation, is rarely more than 60% of those eligible to cast their ballot. In some cases there has been less than a 40% turnout. Equally alarming is the fact that in numerous cases we find citizens who do not know the name of their Congressional representative!

As previously noted, the Greek philosopher Aristotle three centuries B.C. pointed out the intrinsic tendency for people to form self interest groups to promote their narrow agendas. This tendency emphasizes the problem of single issue groups pursuing one topic or narrow theme without regard to adverse effects on the entire body politic. Such single-minded and unwavering approach in a heterogeneous population consisting of myriad concepts regarding governance and economics indicates an authoritative approach to governance and an affront to democracy. The very essence of republican rule is to solve problems which require compromise as a way to find middle ground acceptable to the vast majority of our citizenry – not what a single district desires.

Currently our approach to selecting congressman from gerrymandered districts is disposed to invite, permit and maintain this anomaly for self interest groups. A strong argument can be made that members of congress should represent statewide interests as opposed to cloistered and insulated segments of the public. Election on a statewide basis would better guarantee political positions on governance and economics as well as to reflect the interests of the public at large rather than a segregated group in a gerrymandered district.

It is only when the government and/or a socioeconomic system begins to favor some or a few over others or the public at large that correctional changes become mandatory provided a republic is to be preserved. Therefore it is necessary to provide guarantees by legislation or constitutional amendment to preserve equal protection and opportunity for all. There should be no equivocation that discriminatory laws, regulations and practices should be legally prohibited. We have made major inroads for these protections but many loopholes persist. It is time for a comprehensive declaration of individual rights to be assured by constitutional means.

Could it be agreed that every person requires education and reasonable health and vitality to take advantage of whatever opportunities may be available to them? Only by universal provisions that make these prerequisites possible, with no exceptions or exclusions, can opportunities avail themselves to all who seek it. It is the nation which becomes stronger when all individual citizens have an open path to these necessities. If a few do not avail themselves to what is an open and equal opportunity let it be their choice or ability, not governmental or societal restraints. Freedom and opportunity are the basic ingredients which allow and promote progress in all human affairs, however they can't guarantee it.

As perceptive as our constitutional framers were they were not clairvoyant and could not have foreseen the prodigious growth and expansion of the nation as well as the monumental developments in technology and the advent of economic globalization. We should not be immobilized in our thinking and fail to recognize the magnitude which time and changes in world and national conditions have necessitated updates in our governance. Continental isolation is no longer a factor in our national practices and our international policies. Among the many reasons are electronic communication, jet airplanes, and computerized means of research, satellites and transmission of information all of which make distance irrelevant.

The focus of freedom in modern times includes social and economic justice which permits and guarantees opportunity for both. In an economic sense the boom and bust syndrome of unrestrained financial and economic endeavor requires answers. The 19th and early 20th centuries' versions of capitalism provide us with the lessons that all endeavors require a social conscience in a republic. The near innate tendency of many financial operations and ventures to pursue financial rewards exclusively without reasonable regard for national interests should never be accepted. Necessary and reasonable regulations to protect the public welfare and safety will not interfere with the continuance of a truly free market system when there is a social conscience at the helm.

All human endeavors in a world where populations are exploding require a social conscience to protect the economy and environment on which our very lives depend. Africa alone, within three or four decades is likely to have a population twice that of the United States. The world population continues to increase exponentially and people everywhere seek the same things – security, liberty, opportunity and a healthy environment. It is our nation that must provide an example for the world to illustrate how a republic can work for everyone.

The globalization of economies alone dictates the need for new approaches in how and with whom we partner but even more important is how we protect and ensure our governmental independence. Numerous international corporations owe only token allegiance to any nation – only to the degree necessitated by their business interests. Corporations which are owned or capitalized by governments – state capitalism – have no allegiance to any government except the one that owns them. Their single and only interest in any other nation is how much profit they can extract from them. It is a modern version of the old system of national mercantilism. All corporations should be required to vow allegiance to the constitution of the state in which they are incorporated and to the U.S. Constitution.

Numerous attempts have been made to sound this warning. "The most powerful corporate forces have tightened their control of both the state and the media in the interests of aggressively promoting a pro-business agenda at the expense of other groups. The consequences of neoliberalism and its program of deregulation, tax breaks for the wealthy, military buildup, cutback of social programs, and the widening of class divisions are increasingly evident in the new millennium. As the new century unfolds, globalized societies confront the specter of ever-increasing corporate and military power, worsening social conditions for the vast majority, and sporadic mixtures of massive apathy and explosive conflict."[***]

If any citizen should think that a creeping, imminent peril does not exist for democracies they should take a close look at the governments of the world today. There are now more people living in authoritative type governments than in democratic regimes. Authoritative governments are not only alive and well today but the growth of democracy faces an uphill battle. This truth is largely due to several reasons including

---

[***] Douglas Kellner "The Media and Social Problem" in George Ritzer,[ed] "Handbook of Social Problems" third edition by Robert Heiner.

long traditions and social cultures, uneducated masses of people and the advent in recent decades of state capitalism. The oil rich Near Eastern countries, Russia and China are glowing examples but there are examples in our own hemisphere of the globe as well.

The public media, to a substantial degree, has been hindered by the necessity for advertising, their main source of income. Obviously the profit motive must be considered for survival. But the days when the public could depend upon realistic edification or look forward to muckraker journalism to expose both private and public misdeeds appears to be over to a substantial degree. This is an arena of vast importance for the formation of public sentiment and therefore of significant importance for a republic. The bottom line question becomes how to resolve the clash between the necessity for profit to maintain a viable business enterprise and the public necessity to receive factual and verifiable information.

The corporate ownership linkages in the public media are a maze which requires a cadre of specialists in law, accounting and finance to unravel. The globalization of business enterprises is a fact of today's world. Corporations such as Microsoft, General Electric, AT&T, AOL, Time Warner, Viacom, GE/NBC etc. – the list goes on of corporations doing business in all industrialized nations of the world. This only illustrates the problem of citizens in a republic, or elsewhere, to receive the kind of unfiltered information to aid them in the selection of their representatives and to make their choices on many ballot initiatives. Some media outlets are obvious propaganda machines while others take a more subdued approach. Only public television makes a valid attempt to present straightforward information.

The preservation of individual liberties now faces a most imposing barrier and we must find ways to preserve it, or it will be forever lost. How important is an educated population to the preservation of freedom and to a vigorous economy? Can freedom and ignorance coexist in a republic? Recall President Thomas Jefferson's admonition that to expect ignorance and freedom is to expect something that never was and never will be. It is vital that we thoroughly recognize this basic fact and act vigorously on it. Human knowledge, good health and equal opportunity are triplet requirements for a vigorous society, economic vitality and political involvement – in capsule form the required ingredients of a republic. When we consider personal and family safety, and a true justice system we are brought to the realization that these are the essential features for which we have instituted and pursued our form of government.

A universal and effective educational system is not only indispensable to our republic but is also indispensable to a growing and flourishing economy. An educated public is also required in order to preserve and manage a representative government. Recall Thomas Paine's warning "reason obeys itself, and ignorance submits to whatever is dictated to it." The justice system is also strengthened by an informed public. In short, education is the animating spirit for human liberty and opportunity. It is only as an educated, healthy and vigorous people that we can maintain ourselves as the foremost nation in the world and preserve democracy in a rapidly changing and threatening world.

An essential component for the preservation of our republic is the value system as practiced by society. Our value system drives our lives, directing what we do and what we place on the list of the most important things in our daily lives. Are we a star struck society? Have we developed cultural values where only notoriety or wealth equals public acclaim? How a society spends its time and money becomes a mirror to its values. Seriously contemplate the things that society emphasizes the most. Do most of these enrich life and enhance the human condition? Do they promote health and well-being, and do they consider the future and improve society? Do they promote parenting and family life? Can we honestly face admitting to the real answer to those questions? Should we prepare and present a model social standard for public edification and consideration?

Every society conducts itself according to various stimuli. The stimuli are so numerous that many volumes have been written to address them. Suffice it to say simply, that there are many positive and negative contributions to the list. If our aim is to improve our governance it would seem wise to search for means of introducing as many positive elements as possible. Universal public education is certainly among them. Various ad hoc commissions of leading scholars, divided into the various fields of public interest, should be assembled on a bi-annual basis to assess and propose ideas for public consideration. Our nation is blessed with many people in all areas of public concern and we are not wise to disregard the potential for their contributions. Their proposals could be proffered to any public representatives who deemed the proposals to be advantageous to the public welfare. Public representatives are obligated to instruct and inform as well as to listen.

An educated public, as Thomas Jefferson told us, is a fundamental requirement to preserve freedom. How do we compare with other nations regarding academic attainment? By recent accounts we do not rank among the world's elite in many fields of education. What has happened to result in such a fundamental change?

Notwithstanding the current situation we are still considered the foremost nation in the world. This strange paradox has evolved, for the most part during the past three or four decades. It is our public representatives who must address this problem and provide the means for universal public education. One course of action to amend the process is to restore true representative government so that it becomes the agent for progress and not a figurehead which is held hostage to campaign finances. Since we have drifted into a situation where money buys access and influence we cannot help but see the erosion not only of education but of democracy. The officeholders are left with a dilemma because it is an impossibility to truly serve two masters. The usual remedy is to pass some needed law but insert the inevitable exceptions, a subsidy or an exemption.

In the course of human history, of the millions of people who fought for liberty, most of them perished in the process. Their lives were lost but their ideas and cause never lost and they never will – the essential qualities of humanity decree it! Making great and consequential improvements in our republic will constitute a new chapter in the history of our government. To do so is likely to be a long and arduous task but recall that the founding of our nation did not come easily. The creation of a more perfect union is worth our unceasing efforts. Recall the words of Martin Luther King – "a time comes when silence is betrayal".

With that central point as a launching pad let us examine to some degree the other five of the six goals of our Constitution. Let us do this with the criteria of liberty in a more perfect union as guidelines. It can lead us to some profitable answers.

Odd as it may seem at first to say so, one of the most distinctive things about humanity, one of the things most conducive to civilization, and one of the things potentially most important for the safety, liberty and flourishing of human individuals, is law. I mean law in the sense of "law of the land", law as framed by legislatures and applied by judges, law as what organizes and regulates interpersonal and institutional relationships. Without it what we have is merely a state of nature, where might is right and we get what we can and suffer if we cannot.

Ideas That Matter, A. C. Grayling

CHAPTER 3

To Establish Justice

"When people begin to ignore human dignity, it will not be long before they began to ignore human rights."
G.K. Chesterton, All is Grist.

It is by its justice system that you gain a consequential insight into a nation's value system and its approach and attitude for human dignity and equality. The establishment of a true and proficient justice system is an indispensable cornerstone of democracy and our constitutional framers were enlightened indeed to place the requirement of justice first following the goal of forming a more perfect union. It speaks to the vital role that a justice system occupies in a free society. The root causes of the American Revolution grew out of failures of English justice. Experience with King George III had shown that monarchies had little tolerance for public justice, especially with respect to the colonies.

Equality under law is a meaningless concept without establishing a true justice system to enforce it and upon which a free society rests. Without a true justice system individual freedom, opportunity and security are obstructed resulting in a loss of personal initiative, social achievement and progress. If rights become determined by factors such as social class, political influence, wealth, birthright, religion, ideology or chicanery, true justice no longer exists – because true justice is blind. A comprehensive examination of a nation's justice system requires consideration of the entire socioeconomic and political structure of the country as all play a vital role. This treatise is intended to address only some salient factors.

As mankind evolved from family clans and tribes into joint societies, it became evident that many rules of conduct were required to direct and control individual actions. The Hammurabi code of laws of a Babylonian King in the 18th century BC still shows its influence on modern day justice systems. From that rudimentary beginning, today's justice system is confronted by the astounding complexities of modern commerce and social interactions.

In a republic a justice system is faced with much greater difficulties than in regimes where all law emanates from a central source – a monarch or dictator. The dictates of liberty requires that many factors receive due consideration since in the absence of such criteria as objectivity, equity, social consequences, essential legal procedural requirements and constitutional safeguards, justice would lose focus of its purpose. An effective system of justice in a republic must address and encompass the entire spectrum of an extremely diverse and complicated society. Consider, for example, the many factors which pervade the social structure beginning with domestic relations, social interactions both criminal and civil, commerce and economic activity. It is easy to see that the administration of justice touches and affects our lives in all that we do.

This extremely sketchy portrayal of the breadth and impact of our justice system is meant to portray the daunting and seemingly impossible task to achieve it in practical situations. And it does something more, it tells us to select the most qualified practioners and to install greater safeguards in all public endeavors which rely upon people, because failures can be expected in any human system – perfection is not a human attribute.

The founding principles of our democratic justice system have their origin in the Declaration of Independence, "we hold these truths to be self-evident, that all men are created equal, that they are endowed by their creator with certain unalienable rights, that among these are life, liberty, and the pursuit of happiness." These principles were preconditions of our legal system on which the new nation would base its justice system but would face many hurdles to put in practice. This was the first time in history that the inherent dignity and worth of the individual had been officially engraved into the fabric of government. It is therefore set forth as a requisite for a justice system and a more perfect union. Recognition of the inherent dignity and social equality of all people becomes an indispensable and basic requirement for a justice system in a democracy.

Rendering justice encounters numerous questions and must always consider and assess consequences on individual rights and freedoms juxtaposed with societal requirements. Citizenship in a republic carries with it an obligation and responsibility such as understanding and respecting societal practices that recognize the rights of others. In a democratic society there is no such thing as unconditional freedom since every freedom and every right creates a corresponding obligation to respect the same right and freedom for others. The justice system requires observation of this social necessity.

Dispensing justice in modern society is an ominous and pressure packed task. Cases brought before the courts cover the entire spectrum of human activity. The magnitude and complexity of the entire sphere of American jurisprudence plainly exhibits the necessity for highly trained and professional practitioners. No judge can possess such comprehensive knowledge – without a doubt it is more demanding than what is required by any corporate CEO. Adjudication of cases in law and equity requires not only highly proficient judges but a variety of specialists, advisers and assistants who have become indispensable in today's complex society.

It would be reasonable to expect that very high personal and professional standards would be established as qualifications for all of these judicial offices. Although practices have varied greatly from state to state, interestingly enough in a few cases, the qualification may be less for a justice of the peace than an office clerk in a state or federal court.

Fortunately the era of the JP has substantially ended. Our earlier ideas of democracy indicated that public election of judges was in order but our historical experience does not bear out the veracity of this concept. Public election of judges without requirements for specified professional qualifications appears questionable at best. The vetting process is left to the voter. In theory recall provisions purportedly offered some protection but again the historical facts indicate otherwise.

Our democracy has been an incremental process and has by necessity evolved in its attempts to preserve and enhance its fundamental elements. Has our governmental organization which was designed to carry out this assignment for the establishment of justice been up to the task? Within the scope of our political history and considering the processes put forward in each of the states we have seen that judges, or those who have acted in a judicial capacity, have come to the bench in myriad ways. Whether the selection has been by popular election or by political appointment there has been too little legal prescription regarding qualifications in many of our states.

Concerning the more prestigious courts, such as the top state and federal courts, there have been more worthy examples of professional practice. But in these sectors also there have been some instances where appointments have been made with considerations other than legal qualifications. The appointment of judges and the qualifications for judicial office is an area of our governance that has received too little attention considering their vital role in our governance.

The general public is rarely informed sufficiently to make intelligent choices in the election of judges. Polling results display a confirming amount of enthusiasm. On the federal level the selection of judges has tended to be a question of congruency of socio-economic ideology between the judicial candidate and the appointing authority. But consider the reasons which our founding fathers gave, in the face of great personal danger, to break away from Great Britain. In the Declaration of Independence they declared a set of grievances pointing to the English monarch, King George III, who appointed judges subject to his will and generally obstructed justice including denying benefits of trial by jury.

His "judges" did his bidding; with little to guide their opinions while owing their position to his discretion. Is there a miniscule similarity between the appointment systems? In our republic the separation of powers doctrine gives our courts a high degree of independence and judges have a written constitution, statutes and precedents as guides – all of these are fundamental strengths of a democracy.

To escape the dictatorial actions of a monarchy our governmental organization was based upon the principle of separation of powers thereby preventing the judicial branch from becoming subservient to either the executive or the legislative branches. Seemingly this was a stroke of genius and in many respects it has come close to achieving that objective. But has time and experience exposed some problem areas? History is replete with endeavors to influence the judiciary and almost without exception the appointment of judges at the highest levels has been to select those whose political and socioeconomic views coincide with those of the appointing authority – the president.

This practice appears, in some measure, to diminish the purpose of separation of powers. The president's only hurdle is the consent of the United States Senate. When the two branches are headed by the same party a path is open to shape future national policy. Emblematic of this situation are the several instances where the change of one judge has witnessed a change in the meaning of the Constitution – the Constitution didn't change but one judge did.

The ultimate steward of our legal system is the Supreme Court. It should be obvious that membership in this crucial body should be reserved for the most erudite scholars available. This special position demands the most learned in constitutional law, philosophy, economics, sociology and U. S. history. Plainly no one could become masters in all of these disciplines but it reveals the breath of subjects on which a thorough and valid understanding of constitutional law depends.

Mistakes of judgment especially at this level of the justice system have extremely serious consequences and when those mistakes have their roots in personal biases they degrade the value of democracy. Here again history can be a guide. Our nation has been served by several truly outstanding jurists and many others who would earn a strong passing grade. Unfortunately there have been several who didn't belong on the court. The bottom line question is, can we do better? If we only keep doing the same thing as we have done in the past and expect different results we are guilty of performing folly.

Every observer of this arena of our governance is aware of attempts to manipulate the court. History records a notorious example involving the Dred Scott case in 1857 which held that the litigant, Dred Scott, a slave, could not sue for freedom because "he wasn't a citizen!" President Buchanan was observed, and later documented, to have discussed the case before-hand with Chief Justice Taney. This resulted in then Senator William Seward, to remark "the coalition between the executive and Justice Department to undermine the national legislature and the liberties of the people" and that the court "forgot that judicial usurpation is more odious and intolerable than any other among the manifold practices of tyranny."*

There should be no surprise that such incidents have occurred; after all it is a human institution! Do we ask whether presidents seek the most highly qualified jurist available for appointment? Or do they tend to seek someone who shares their political and socioeconomic concepts? The answer to this last question is exactly what we should expect because the system predicts the result. Virtually any person would do the same thing.

Realistically we must accept the fact that it is to be expected for political leaders to appoint those whose views coincide with their own. No one would expect the president to do the opposite. Such action is only natural and does not infer necessarily any nefarious intent or purpose. Most anyone would follow a course of action which they believe is right and good for the country. However it is to guard against the imperfections of humanity that democratic safeguards are meant to address. To remove temptations will not be a cure for duplicity or guile

---

*   "Seward" by Walter Stahr

but to remove temptations is progress toward our objective to improve our governance, the justice system and our republic.

Questions arise from this procedure regarding assumptions that the appointing authority not only has good intentions but will be correct in evaluating what is best for the country. Perhaps the president will be correct – in many cases. But is there a better way? There appears to be general agreement for a merit system in the selection of judges at all levels. There are 33 states and the District of Columbia which choose some judges through this appointment process. In general, national legal associations such as the American Bar Association and the American Judicature Society oppose the election of judges. A preponderance of judicial scholars agrees that some type of merit appointment is preferable.

Currently judicial selection in the federal court system and several progressive states utilize boards of selection which submit names of the highly qualified candidates to the appointing authority. The problem which persists is the lack of some uniformity throughout the nation for legal, if not constitutional, guidelines and requirements. In addition to the appointment process there is a problem of salaries which excludes many highly qualified candidates from submitting their names for appointment. Justices of the Supreme Court receive less salary than many skilled workers and technicians. As a partner in a major law firm the remuneration could be 20 times that figure, or more.

The vital nature of our judiciary requires our best efforts to formulate the best organization and procedures to accomplish its mission. To find a better way we must examine the major factors. This entails consideration of better and uniform procedures for appointment, a more appropriate remuneration, a possible modification of tenure, more stringent requirements for decisions of constitutionality and perhaps a greater separation of this function of government from the hubbub and political culture of Washington DC.

Ingenious as the separation of powers doctrine is and as well as the system has worked it has also shown some imperfections. These imperfections have evolved from practical experiences including the appointment process which, if ignored, interferes with the courts' impartiality, independence and its public acceptance. Common sense tells us that to expect absolute judicial impartiality is unrealistic. Adopting a rational approach in our efforts to achieve it however is within our ability, at least to the extent that the mind of mankind is capable. The answers we seek consist of designing the most effective procedures, requirements and organization to ensure a bona fide judicial system and its continuance.

A continuing complaint directed at our courts involves the resulting effect of their decisions declaring laws unconstitutional and thereby indirectly engaging in legislative activity. Since the public has little effective recourse in such cases it would seem wise to initiate some corrective measures which we will subsequently explore.

The Supreme Court of the United States took upon itself in Marbury v. Madison the authority to declare unconstitutional duly enacted laws of Congress and approved by the president. Although there is no explicit provision for this power stated in the Constitution it appears to be a logical result of adjudicated questions. It is certainly a logical power but a highly precarious practice for the Supreme Court to possess. However such authority is essential protection to ensure that laws remain congruent with the meaning and intent of the Constitution. We find in the Federalist papers LXXIII a statement that it was the province of the courts to interpret laws. Also Congress has the authority to reenact a law with sufficient modifications to overcome the courts objections.

Such court authority however has elicited charges of assuming the power to legislate – a power specifically assigned to Congress, contradicting the doctrine of separation of powers. It may be forcefully argued that the court's rulings in a number of cases reflect the needs of the nation. But the question still remains whether the courts or Congress and the president are the appropriate and publicly responsible bodies to answer that question. A possible remedy might be a requirement that the court, finding a statute unconstitutional, should be required to refer the matter back to Congress for correction and clarification along with their reasoning of its unconstitutionality. If such a procedure was required the onus would be placed where it should be, on representatives of the people. If Congress and the president fail to take action or make a timely reply the court's ruling would have to stand.

Should Congress be allowed to overturn a Supreme Court ruling of unconstitutionality by a two thirds vote of each house, perhaps with the president's approval? This is the same requirement required to overturn a presidential veto. Or would a three fourths majority be more definitive? At any rate some reasonable recourse should be provided.

To further exasperate the dilemma is the fact that unconstitutionality of a statute is accomplished by a simple majority vote. A 5 to 4 decision does not inspire confidence for that decision. This is further irritated by the fact that several 5 to 4 decisions have subsequently been overturned by identical 5 to 4 decisions! To an unbiased observer, the lay citizen, it appears only common sense if a given law is unconstitutional such a fact should be identified by competent judges. If a decision of this magnitude depends upon a judges socioeconomic and/or political views then the question of constitutionality is actually a legislative decision not a legal one.

Would a constitutional amendment be a better way to clarify the situation? An amendment could specifically grant the Supreme Court power to decide questions of constitutionality and specify a requirement for a two thirds vote on such matters. Obviously this would mean that six of the nine justices would be required for such a decision – a clear majority which reasonable people can accept.

Another approach could be to increase the number of justices to 12. In this event every decision would require at least a 7 to 5 decision or by specific constitutional requirement a two thirds, 8 to 4, decision would be required on cases of constitutionality. Under any circumstance a declaration of unconstitutionality should be an obvious decision for an unbiased, professionally experienced and competent jurist. An alternate approach as previously mentioned, could be a requirement to resubmit the law to Congress with the court's reasoning for its unconstitutionality. Such a referral would be required to be answered by Congress and re-signed by the president within a reasonable time.

The prestige of the Supreme Court is further hindered by decisions which are predictable. In many cases is it ever reasonably certain how a particular judge will rule on specific cases? Questions of this sort point to the fact that better procedural methods of appointment, higher requirements for judicial training, a possible different look at tenure along with greater physical separations between the courts and other branches of government as well as more stringent requirements for decisions regarding constitutionality should be considered.

Let us explore some ideas that might better serve to ensure a competent and independent judiciary. History is replete with examples of powerful kingdoms that failed to survive due to factors revolving around internal conflicts involving political power and personal aggrandizement. In the absence of a court of competent jurisdiction with constitutional powers, such internal conflicts invariably develop into internal chaos and the loss of hope for national unity. A nation's justice system is essential to cope with such conflicts which seem to be ever present in human affairs. In short, our judicial system is a key ingredient which binds our form of governance together. The requirement of an honest and competent justice system has been clearly demonstrated throughout history.

In the popular mind the only prerequisite for a judge is to be a lawyer. A lawyer and a judge are two entirely different professions. Lawyers may specialize in literally scores of legal services required in modern society. Innumerable volumes have been written about these various avenues of legal service. To be sure a top jurist must have a sound legal background. It is equally true that a top jurist should be no stranger to economics and economic history, sociology and American political history, particularly as that history covers the history of justice in this nation. All of this must be the foundation for an intellectually astute and ethical person who aspires to protect human rights and protect a republic.

For the sake of national security we established a National Military Academy to ensure that this nation was protected by professional military leadership. It has proven to be a wise decision. In a like manner it was deemed necessary to establish a National Naval Academy. Another wise decision made necessary to protect our shores and our maritime commerce. In a like manner we established the Coast Guard Academy and the United States Air Force Academy. The security of our nation is well served by these establishments made necessary to produce competent professional leadership. Is our justice system less important or vital? Consider historical lessons detailing the collapse of great empires due to internal conflicts – conflicts which a constitutionally empowered justice system could resolve. Be reminded that many earlier kingdoms collapsed more from internal problems than by foreign enemies! Our justice system is the backbone of our internal defense system – our internal Army, Navy and Air Force.

Would it not be sensible to create a national academy for postgraduate work devoted to training candidates in the field of jurisprudence to help develop professional jurists? Any devotee of democracy would be hard-pressed to specify a profession which has greater impact on social justice and therefore human liberty and freedom. Our social order having a base of ethical and moral standards should insist also on justice in its economic and political institutions.

It seems there has always been a suspicion in various sections of the nation regarding the federal government's usurpation of power with a corresponding loss of liberty. Observance of and adherence to the Constitution is our warranty for protection against such a transfer of governmental power. However, to assuage these apprehensions and to place another safeguard for the long-term protection of republican rule would it be appropriate to allow the Supreme Court [if constituted by 12 top-flight jurists] to examine and explore the constitutionality of specified practices of any governmental operation when requested by a super majority vote, say 55 affirmative votes, of the Senate or a three/fifths vote of the House of Representatives? Or, in a like manner, the president could request an examination of a specific practice of any governmental operation or a particular practice of Congress? In each case these petitions should contain specific areas of concern with sufficient supporting backup for the court to decide the efficacy of the requests.

As long as our governmental hierarchy, the President, the House of Representatives, the United States Senate and ultimately the Supreme

Court can be made subject to the public will, the government must be more powerful and be the ultimate authority for society and for commerce and industry. In spite of its many foibles, which we the people have the power to correct, our democratic system is far superior and more desirable than any other system where governmental power rests in a single religion, a particular class, in a single person or an economic order.

A fundamental principle of our federal system is the separation of powers. Our efforts therefore should be to make real that ingenious concept. One approach could be to separate the Supreme Court from the political culture of the nation's capital. Washington DC is dominated by the presence of the White House, and the Capitol building housing the United States Senate and the House of Representatives. The machinations attendant to national government and administration are the predominant elements of the capital city. It is their operations which swirl continuously and absorbs public attention. This circumstance establishes a political culture which has been ingrained for well over two centuries. This political culture is a contradiction to thoughtful and independent jurisprudence. The courts operate as a deliberative function and the never ending political maneuvering on Capitol Hill is hardly compatible.

Anyone who has lived for some length of time in a cloistered setting realizes how that culture becomes unique and separated from the real world around them. A separate location for the Supreme Court as the chief player would result in a better climate and atmosphere for deliberation. This would be just another safeguard to provide greater independence.

Conceivably a geographical separation would provide greater incentive and stimulus for unfettered decisions. Additionally if the location were more centrally located in the nation the citizenry would be given a greater feeling of confidence in the independence and impartiality of the court. Recall that the only reason Washington DC was selected as the capital was due to its central location of the 13 colonies in 1789! Why shouldn't the same reason apply today?

Perhaps some modification of the appointing process also would be in order. An ad hoc panel of the nation's top academic legal professors, the American Bar Association, the American Judicature Society, US historians, economists and sociologists could be impaneled as needed to certify a list of eligible candidates for the various federal judgeships. The president could then select one for consideration by the Senate. Or perhaps the Senate by a 3/5 majority vote should first reduce such a certified list to five or seven candidates from which the president could make a selection. Could an approach of this type help to reduce partisan conflicts as well as developing a court with less bias and predilection to rule according to script? A process of this nature could reduce an appointee's feelings of obligation to any person, group or ideology.

Other matters of primary importance are tenure, and the number of justices on the Supreme Court. On these matters there are of course numerous opinions and no absolute answers. However the fact that serious questions have arisen and history points to some potential problems gives rise to serious considerations for possible improvement.

Regarding tenure the Constitution provides Supreme Court judges with tenure conditioned only with the requirement of "good behavior" which historically has meant lifelong tenure. There is no constitutional or legal definition for good behavior. Legislation or constitutional amendment should define "good behavior" to prohibit political activity, contacts with federal administrative or legislative officials and with attorneys or representatives of parties scheduled to try cases before the federal courts. This would have to be imposed in such a manner as not to impede any transmission of vital information required by the court. In the past there have been instances too numerous to count of contacts between congressmen, presidents, senators, special interest representatives, and attorneys who are scheduled to try cases before the court. It is a rarity for a Supreme Court justice to recuse themselves from a case where such contact has been made.

A lifetime appointment is aimed at establishing an assurance for independence which is vital for the autonomy of the court. At the same time there is the potential for superannuated justices. The notion that Supreme Court judges rarely die and never retire is ascribed to President Thomas Jefferson. Regardless of its veracity it does elicit a potential problem. To guard against such a potential perhaps a 20 year appointment may be a consideration with the provision that a 10 year extension could be in order provided there were medical assurances of physical and mental capabilities. Certainly today with the rapid pace and major changes in the world and our nation there is a vastly new and dynamic situation which challenges judges. Their health, energy and mental acuity are paramount. The nation's interest should never have to depend upon a justice who is not totally competent to serve for whatever reason.

If ensuring justice is truly one of the cornerstones of democracy, and it surely is a most vital part of its foundation, the presidential power to grant pardons should be more clearly defined as to its scope and purpose. The use of this power for political reasons is inimical to justice necessitating a procedure which requires public notice and input. Requirements to provide an open and clear procedure for the granting of pardons should not eliminate this presidential prerogative. It has a rightful place in a democratic society. Miscarriages of justice are not a totally rare occasion and therefore should be remedied. But the prerogative to correct these occurrences should not, in turn, open a path for political duplicity.

Our political history has shown us that a few presidents have granted pardons to political friends or associates to oblige, for whatever reason, as a quid pro quo. Democracy is never served when there is an invitation to allow illegal conduct or activity to be excused. In our present day situation the "behind closed doors" schemes of political parties are to be expected and even excused. However, they should never be allowed to circumvent the law. These are matters for which our courts have been created to resolve.

It appears that most citizens immediately think of the courts, then judges and finally lawyers when the subject of our justice system is broached. And, if public opinion can be used as a gauge, few seem to be given an extraordinarily high rating! Why is this? Such a general concept appears somewhat atypical since a large majority of the personnel holding positions in these professions are highly trained, competent and carry out their task in a professional manner – and in numerous cases they are exposed to serious personal risks. Unfortunately, prejudice, stratagems and even corruption have, on rare occasion, found a way into various parts of our justice system including law enforcement, prosecution as well as the courts. Legal technicalities have resulted infrequently also in a miscarriage of justice.

Without question there have been too many examples in our justice system of incompetence, political chicanery, racial bias and rulings on purely ideological grounds. They are not the rule however, and they do not define the courts or the legal profession. When much depends upon and is expected from something any error or ethical breach becomes an exaggerated example. It seems to be the case of one rotten apple spoiling the entire bushel. Every field of human activity has been defiled or embarrassed by some member overstepping the bounds of ethical or moral behavior – including religion.

Another basic and vital ingredient of our justice system is law enforcement at all levels of government. Law enforcement is the advanced guard of defense in our justice system. If there are any segments in the governmental hierarchy where high professional standards are necessary, and there are several such segments, it is in the realm of law enforcement. Whether it be a city, county, state or the federal government, professional training and high standards for qualification are essential. It is in this component of our justice system where information is derived which is used by attorneys and the courts. Although these remarks apply principally in the criminal realm it is the area of the justice system which most directly touches the lives of most citizens.

Police agencies play a vital role in civil matters as well, which requires specialization and expertise in a variety of disciplines, all of which become mandatory to dispense true justice. Far too little attention has been directed to this critical component of our justice system. There must be greater emphasis on higher entry qualifications, training and educational requirements. This is a demanding and dangerous profession and, like all professions, it requires people with particular and distinct qualifications. It is the sector of the justice system which the average citizen is most likely to encounter and is most likely to depend upon. Many citizens will likely judge the justice system in this way alone.

In a republic a fundamental truth basic to its preservation and improvement involves having an involved public with knowledge and understanding regarding all sectors of our governance as to their specific responsibilities and an insistence on their performance. In the last analysis it falls to the voting public to perform this function. In any analysis, in every area of the justice system, education and high entry requirements, good organization and comprehensive constitutional requirements are paramount to the establishment of justice for the republic we seek.

This generation, this time in our history, finds us at a crucial stage in the march of mankind to develop and maintain that more perfect union. In so doing we may save the last best hope for democracy on earth. What is the destiny of humanity if we do not seek to continually develop better environments, reform our governmental practices and organization, strive to develop an improved society and institute better living conditions? Are we not hardwired to search always for what our creation promised? Is this not what real justice is all about?

When Confucius was asked what would be the first thing that he would do if he were to lead the state – his never-to-be fulfilled dream – he said, "rectify the language!" This is wise. This is subtle. As societies grow decadent, the language grows decadent, too. Words are used to disguise, not to illuminate, action: you liberate a city by destroying it. Words are used to confuse, so that at election time people will solemnly vote against their own interests ..... Is rectification of our system possible for us?

The Day the American Empire Ran Out of Gas,
Gore Vidal.

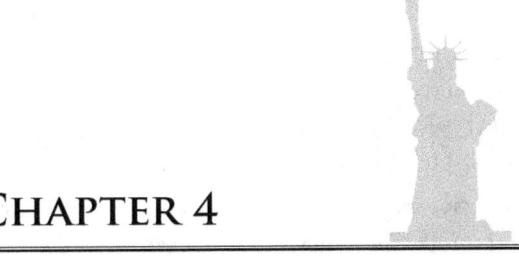

CHAPTER 4

Insure Domestic Tranquility

"Every civilization is, among other things, an arrangement for domesticating the passions and setting them to do useful work." Aldous Huxley, Collected Essays

Have you ever had a serious discussion about domestic tranquility? Would it be presumptuous to speculate that the vast majority of citizens rarely, if ever, consider domestic tranquility as a requisite part of their lives? Or, if it is considered, would it be only in connection with their personal or family situation? Only a casual thought is required to make us realize that domestic tranquility is essential in virtually everything we do – in making a living, in our social life and for domestic safety and enjoyment. It is the required element for the assurance of a safe, functional social order and desirable living conditions.

National cohesion, social and individual achievement, personal well-being and economic progress all hinge upon domestic tranquility. This is what our constitutional framers understood and therefore targeted as an objective for the new republic. Their reference to the term "domestic tranquility" took the broad view as it applied to societal requirements as opposed to a limited reference to family concerns. This broader view points the way for social growth and advancement in all fields of human endeavor.

The same concept is as true today as it was in the 18th century. However, the means and requirements to achieve it have undergone a prodigious evolution since the Constitution was written. Unfortunately there have been always those who insist upon muddying the waters, ignoring and violating the basic rules for societal living. Since the time of Cain there have been those who seek to live by few ethical, moral or social standards. Similarly, there are always people who seek personal gain or unfair advantage whenever or however they find the opportunity. Effective enforcement of social rules regarding public health, welfare and safety becomes mandatory in a civilized world. Domestic tranquility depends on equal, open and fair opportunity throughout society and mutual respect for everyone. Domestic tranquility has much to do with public confidence and respect for law and order, our environs and for our governments.

To emphasize the difficulty of achieving and maintaining domestic tranquility try to envision society in the late 1700s. By any constituent feature 21st-century America has become totally divergent from that bygone era. And just as the United States has gone through a metamorphosis so has the world in which we live. Recognition of this change is essential to accept in order to adapt ourselves to new ways which will ensure safety, liberty, opportunity and social justice. The type of individualism which was possible in that day has no place in modern society. Individualism today must find different avenues for expression and its possibilities can have even greater vistas to explore and contribute to the social order. The great advances in the fields of science and technology have been made possible as the result of an assurance of a social order in which numerous individuals have been able to follow their dreams and utilize their talents – individualism.

A local constable and a night watchman may have sufficed to provide domestic tranquility in 1790. Cities and towns of that day were small and lifestyles moved at a much slower pace. The fact that most people were personally known throughout an area in that bygone era served as a self policing factor for society. Even the temptations which we know today were not a problem or a distraction at that time. This very brief description is to emphasize the vast difference between providing domestic tranquility in the 1790s and the 21st century. Today the constable has been replaced by a cadre of trained policeman and a network of local, state and federal inspectors and investigators. But social tranquility demands and requires an educated, ethical and law-abiding public who have faith and respect in their republic. Social tranquility requires a humane and principled way of life which results in public safety and human advancement.

Domestic tranquility involves more than maintaining social order, which is basic to that covenant. Maintaining domestic tranquility involves our social values and all that we accept and practice as a way of life – for ourselves, our children and for others. The family unit remains as a basic strength in society. Concepts and beliefs regarding a way of life to embrace civic responsibility begin in early childhood with early education and neighborhood environment playing a central role. Social order alone does not equate to peace of mind and equanimity. Totalitarian regimes mandate social order but they cannot order peace of mind. Peace of mind also requires assurance of safety, opportunity and justice.

Domestic tranquility in a republic must emanate from responsible, ethical and principled public behavior. This type of society is highly important for personal and public advancement and the pursuit of happiness. Freedom carries that kind of responsibility and must be learned in early childhood.

Take a very brief look at our society and its many inter-related components: family, vocations, avocations and leisure time, religion, political and social affiliations, education, etc. – all are impacted by science, technology, government, and the mass media. Each of these, in actuality, impact and influence the others. Education has a profound impact on government and politics, on employment and therefore vocations and the economy and even on religion. These elements of society become the arena in which our social mores become the director.

Now, consider another quick, sketchy look at a few of the social factors or situations which we face in our society. Freedom of speech, racial discrimination, religious discrimination, extreme wealth, extreme poverty, taxation, spare time, gangs, drug use, criminal behavior, the death penalty, civic responsibilities, homosexuality, gender discrimination, human rights, lethal weapons, marriage, family, abortion and so forth – the list goes on. How each of us views, understands and reacts to these and other societal issues forms a perspective which directs the way we live, shaping our social mores or norms, which in turn, develops a national direction, its strength and its future. This becomes our national culture and defines who we are as a people.

Again, comprehensive education, family and neighborhood environment become foundations for our early life experiences and are fundamental to how each of us view ourselves and others, setting a course for how we live our lives. How we live our lives predicts the kind of society and government we will create and demand.

Notwithstanding the colossal changes since 1789 a few very important ingredients for domestic tranquility have remained essentially the same. These social values consist of a belief in individual liberty, individual and family safety, social justice and opportunity for all. The public's commitment to these values is made meaningful through parenting and education to ensure that everyone understands and accepts their role and obligations for the preservation of that society. It becomes a question of educating our human nature for a continuance and improvement of such values. People everywhere, regardless of race and ethnicity, birthplace, ideological persuasion or theological leanings want the same things – safety and comfortable living conditions, good health, social justice, opportunity and liberty, all of which are inextricably connected with domestic tranquility as well as key ingredients of a republic.

Consider what really constitutes the basis for "Americanism" and how it relates to domestic tranquility. First, consider that "Americanism" is a basic motivating factor for most people who seek to come to this country. It is what everyone desires for themselves and their families. All of us spring from ancestors from foreign lands except for American Indians. Our ancestors came here for the very same reasons that people still want when they migrate to this nation – something capsulated in the word "Americanism" which has little to do with geography – it is what this country stands for – it is domestic tranquility encompassing safety, justice, freedom and opportunity which opens the door to entrepreneurism and the pursuit of happiness.

Domestic tranquility is also a fundamental objective of our justice system. The basic aim of justice is to see that everyone obeys the rules of society and thereby provides a safe environment for people to pursue their chosen aims in life. This provides insight to our culture which is an essential ingredient for the development and preservation of a republic. Domestic tranquility, liberty, justice and opportunity are forever interwoven with "Americanism" and are intrinsic motivating characteristics of patriotism. Americanism and patriotism then are not concepts which have anything to do with land or location. To the contrary, they are a way of life devoted to the fundamental desires of humanity – fundamental human rights to which all people aspire and are entitled.

It becomes vital to the continuance of democracy that we never forget or confuse patriotism and Americanism with land or location whether that is a homestead, a city, county or state. All of these are formed by imaginary man-made lines which have been drawn for myriad reasons and circumstances. All of these boundary lines are fictional, made legal by the stroke of a pen, which can and have been altered many times for various reasons. Local and state pride can and does serve many beneficial purposes. The problem arises when they become confused with Americanism and patriotism. When this happens domestic tranquility suffers along with national cohesion.

The human tendency to take pride in their surroundings, their home, neighborhood, school, city or state is an admirable trait. It speaks to creating desirable living conditions, developing social involvement, advancing education and fulfilling life's goals. It is only when such pride becomes confused and distorted turning into boastful swaggering with animosity toward others from a different neighborhood, city or state, that it becomes adverse to the social order. Domestic tranquility depends on and requires keeping our values focused properly and maintaining respect for others – acknowledging the dignity of all people and our commonality and Americanism.

An earlier reference was made to the great disparity between 21st-century United States and the original 13 colonies. In many cases of that day each person, each family, especially those on or near the frontier, of necessity, needed to protect and defend themselves. In many cases family farms were situated where various threats could be encountered. In addition hunting provided a food supply for the family. At that time the requirement of individualism was more of a necessity rather than a choice as a way of life. A comparable circumstance today would be impossible to find. Domestic tranquility to our ancestors was an individual and family (or clan?) affair. This concept is totally different from the concept of our constitutional preamble which was focused essentially on a nation's need for unity and order in society at large and among the various states.

No thinking person can deny that personal safety and family security are basic requirements for a productive life and a stable society. So basic indeed that safety will and has taken precedence over liberty. Social stability – domestic tranquility – is fundamental for the development and conduct of schools, entrepreneurism, commerce, travel, religious practice, social gatherings, entertainment and virtually everything we do in our everyday lives. It is therefore fundamental to achieve and maintain domestic tranquility in order for society to exist as a productive element of a strong nation and to preserve a republic.

We now live in a totally new and different world where every populated place on earth is as near to us time-wise as Concorde, New Hampshire was to Atlanta, Georgia in 1787. For purposes of personal interchange people in France, Britain, Brazil or Germany are as much our neighbors today as New Hampshire and South Carolina were when they agreed to ratify our Constitution. Today's national ethnicity, once principally English, is now a microcosm of the world. American citizens today truly represent humanity, all of whom aspire to that "American dream" made possible by our insistence upon domestic tranquility, opportunity, individual liberty and justice. We are becoming a new "race" of people amalgamating everyone!

Today's threats to domestic tranquility are not from the frontier which has long since been engulfed by our "manifest destiny". Today, threats come from foreign and a few domestic terrorists, rogue nations, monopolistic cartels, development of social stratification, sectarian divisiveness, public apathy and a dwindling understanding and devotion to the basics of our national purpose and founding values. And what are our founding values? They are all in the preamble of the Constitution of the United States! Let us begin anew to define and guarantee our founding values with a new burst of freedom and justice.

There is an abundance of public laws and regulations in various governmental jurisdictions which are intended to protect and defend our social tranquility. In addition there is an array of enforcement methods which constitute our justice system. When we hear of murder, robbery, assault, and drug trafficking that pervade all of our cities along with the possibility for terrorist incursions into our social order we should become doubly aware of how much we rely upon an abundance of public agencies for protection. Even public health can be threatened by the spread of an epidemic of viruses and we must rely upon our public health agencies and scientific resources to protect us. No city or state alone can provide all the means to provide protection from these threats. It is by a nation united that we can prevail. President Abraham Lincoln said it best, "a house divided against itself cannot stand."

To be sure our constitutional framers could not have foreseen the magnitude of such threats but their language is broad enough to cover all these possibilities. It is up to us to make the adjustments to meet changing times and ensure the continuance of our republic. By recognizing that many of the things we do and how we lead our lives in meaningful and productive ways becomes a factor in the social order – domestic tranquility – it becomes evident that what we do as individual citizens has consequences. In a democracy domestic tranquility begins and heavily relies upon individual values and conduct.

Should we not have a thoughtful, intelligent social master plan which points the way to a better tomorrow? Everyone should recognize that we cannot stand still – we either progress or we regress. Our nation is blessed by having scores of people who have spent their lives studying and analyzing social problems, how we live and what our societal difficulties are which result in a great deal of human misery and which becomes a retarding agent for overall social progress. Perhaps a biennial national convention of these professionals could outline proposals of ways and means for all of us to have a goal to consider and look forward to for a better, more satisfying and more rewarding way of life.

However the social process may evolve should it not be influenced intellectually? Is it possible that we are capable of differentiating the good habits and characteristics from those that prove to be negative or detrimental? And on a broader stage can modern communication which introduces and connects discordant cultures, together with international travel and better education bring peoples of the world toward a more uniform world culture which adopts the best traits from all of them?

From a practical point of view it is likely that we will never, certainly in our lifetimes, create and live in a perfect society. But such a fact doesn't mean that an intelligent effort shouldn't be made to inch forward toward that goal. Let us use our social professionals as we do our medical professionals for advice and recommendations. Remember, ideas evolve to meet requirements concerning personal circumstances, living conditions, national issues and the unknowns of the future. If we try, if we put forward willing effort, we will improve and advance our domestic tranquility, not only for ourselves but for generations to come.

Once again let us recall President James Madison's affirmation who told us that only a true republic can govern in a heterogeneous society. It is vital that we heed his instruction and warning. It tells us that our differences will sever our social contract, our union, unless we are capable of developing and maintaining an authentic republic; one that is devoted to liberty, justice and equal opportunity; one where all views can be heard through courteous and respectable discourse, and where decisions can be made on common grounds.

For our nation to grow and progress we, the people, must come to the realization that real contentment, peace of mind and achieving a bona fide pursuit of happiness are all tied to satisfaction that comes from achievement, personal development, friendships, social engagement and being a good neighbor. This realization will coincide with an understanding that great abundance and extravagant consumption are ephemeral gratification only and not a satisfying way of life.

How we employ and utilize our personal freedom results in how we live. In this sense we are the masters of our own fate. In the final analysis our beliefs and activities determines domestic tranquility and whether we can govern ourselves in a republic. It is only common sense to try to have a better way of life. Freedom, when exercised wisely and responsibly becomes that inalienable right which our Creator endowed us and is the catalyst for greatness and for personal fulfillment – if the better side of our nature is allowed to control our actions. That kind of freedom ensures a better life, a better nation, brought about by our domestic tranquility.

Even worse than the not-very-likely prospect of nuclear war – deliberate or by accident – is the economic collapse of our society because too many of our resources have been wasted on the military. The Pentagon is like a black hole; what goes there is forever lost to us, and no wealth is created. Hence, our cities, whose centers are unlivable; our crime rate, the highest in the Western world; the public education system that has given up...... You know the litany.

> The Day the American Empire Ran Out of Gas
> Gore Vidal

CHAPTER 5

Provide for the Common Defense

"The price of freedom is eternal vigilance." Thomas Jefferson.

Without question providing for our common defense is a fundamental requirement of government. It is the strength, effectiveness and reliability of our common defense which is vital for our preservation – preservation in many areas of social and national concern. In this regard we are inclined to first think of military preparedness and our cohesion expressed by patriotism and action, not words, defining our solidarity and resolves to protect our way of life. The strength of our common defense relies on the solidarity of our people but also on awareness of our interdependence as a society as well as mutual devotion to liberty.

Our solidarity finds its basis in commitment to the ideals of our republic. Confidence in a genuine republic committed to liberty has compelled hundreds of thousands to give their lives. When people feel they are a meaningful part of society, which provides them liberty, equal opportunity and justice, they will defend it. The common will of the people is a mighty force.

As a unified nation determined to save our way of life, it becomes incumbent upon everyone to support a common defense. The "common defense" literally means to incorporate everyone into the equation. To achieve a totally effective common defense our internal solidarity fulfills an indispensable component.

But when a society divides into caste-like classes, national cohesion is splintered and national solidarity gravely threatened. This scenario divulges the significant importance of authentic public representation and laws which do not favor any person or organization unless there is a demonstrable and authentic public requirement. We must insist that there is a generic meaning to "equal protection of the laws". Failing this, aspirations of maintaining a republic begins to erode piece by piece and along with it the common will to preserve the nation.

Common defense is not just defense against foreign enemies and it is not limited to military power. It must include a defense against internal failures which threaten our democratic structure and procedures. If the framework for democratic government and the procedures for carrying it out effectively are defiled and corrupted they could represent the most dangerous adversary of all. Great empires of history have withered and collapsed as a result of internal problems. A startling lesson from history is that most national governments have rarely endured more than 200 years! Defending the structure and practices of democracy is just as necessary as maintaining a formidable military establishment. What good would the military be without democracy?

The meaning of common defense therefore is more encompassing than military preparedness alone. The preservation and defense of society encounters a variety of dangers and threats requiring our common defense to include a wide range of factors. Among these are an educated citizenry, a fully coordinated federal administration, an authentic representative government, a social culture based on individual achievement and personal contribution, preeminence in medical and scientific fields , a vibrant economy and domestic manufacturing, astute foreign relations, comprehensive strategic plans, mastery in technology, professionally managed cities, as well as a first-class military preparedness.

Relevant debate emerges regarding how to best provide our national defense. Valid differences can arise on such questions and variables as to the extent and cost as well as to the specific needs and purposes. Finding agreement on specific goals and objectives as well as to determine methods to provide the financial resources required will always necessitate considerate and well-informed debate. Only through well-meaning and informed discussion can appropriate decisions of this nature be made. It should never be the platform for political demagoguery or personal showmanship – other nations have ears!

Our nation has developed numerous federal agencies who are involved in one way or another with national security. But our national defense suffers from a lack of a total integration of the insights and conclusions of all the agencies involved. In each of the operational areas a completely formulated national strategy with specific objectives and coherent operational plans to carry out the intended missions is rarely complete. This becomes apparent when it is revealed that one area of government pursues a path which is not in harmony with another.

Our national defense requires a thorough understanding of the history, culture, economy, internal problems and governmental arrangement and leadership of all the nations with whom our interests intersect. This kind of understanding must be present in several governmental agencies including the State Department, the Defense Department and various command centers as well as the Pentagon, CIA, FBI, Homeland Security, Joint Chiefs, Justice Department and integrated for the White House.

With so many viewpoints, arrived at by different information sources there is bound to be different points of view, perhaps friction and jealousy. With so many entities involved the results emanating from so many talented and experienced players, could actually create turmoil and confusion which, in turn, could be calamitous. A comprehensive examination of this overall structure should be made mandatory.*

---

*   See"The Battle for Peace", by General Tony Zinni [a must read for every American]

Several nations today are coming ever closer to matching us with the means and methods, industrially, technologically, scientifically and educationally to compete, at least in a number of these sectors. A vastly different viewpoint is now required which means that we must comprehend events and conditions from a world point of view rather than just from a national perspective. Additionally we must recognize that these great changes in the world we live in affect the way we live and the way we deal with others.

Warfare can no longer be a matter of choice for there likely will be no celebrating for the winners. Today's reality must recognize and deal with the development of other nations. Our future lies in building strong, binding friendships with all of the Western Hemisphere, with Europe, with African nations, with Malaysia, India and all others who will support the ideals of human liberty. Such a foreign relations approach is not only our best defense but also a potent presentation for the strength of representative government.

Every true American will agree upon the defense of our country and, hopefully, be willing to defend democracy with equal fervor. But we must keep in mind that in international affairs the only stable solution is not for any one side to dominate or subjugate another. Our nation should never be perceived around the world as a bully or a pariah.

In dealing with other nations we must keep in mind and respect the disparity among cultures which have developed and been in place for many centuries. Virtually all other nations have evolved into their present situations, we invented ours. In international affairs both sides must feel a reasonable degree of comfort from the interchange. It is far better to be respected than feared.

What we must learn is that we cannot change the culture of another nation; we haven't been able to change significantly our own! Most of our culture is less than 250 years old and during this time we have been constantly varying and changing as a result of immigrations, international travel and communication technology. During those years we have integrated and Americanized large immigrant infusions of

IS THE UNITED STATES WORTH SAVING?

Irish, Italians, Germans, French, Hebrew, Chinese, Japanese, Arabs and more recently Vietnamese and Mexicans – not to mention Africans who were brought in against their will and American Indians who were able to survive our manifest destiny. All have made significant contributions. The amalgamation of all these people has enriched our culture and our way of life which we call American.

In our busy lives what many Americans fail to fully comprehend and appreciate is how we are perceived around the world. This has a great deal to do with our common defense. Perhaps it also indicates a lack of appreciation for what a republic means to people around the world. Consider Ben Franklin's concept, "America's destiny is not power, but light."

Also consider the remark of an Arab friend of General Tony Zinni following the terrorist attack on the World Trade Towers, "I'm worried that this tragedy could cause America to stop being America. You Americans don't know your power, your influence, and your goodness. Your anger in the retaliation you are about to take is justified. But in doing what you must do to respond to this evil, I hope, for the sake of the world, that you never lose sight of your values and your sense of justice in the actions that you take. The world needs you more than you realize."** These comments illustrate the worldwide importance of maintaining a beacon of liberty and why we should make every effort to enhance and preserve a true republic. The destiny of human liberty in the world is in our hands.

Nations rise and nations fall but rarely has a nation ever entirely changed those whom they have forcibly conquered. History has proved that the human mind will continue to choose and select – and to discard – those things which do not stand the test of time in their culture. We must realize that many cultures date back to the Middle Ages or longer. Our foreign-policy must understand and deal with this fact of life. It is our culture which must promote individual achievement and social involvement. It is in the fields of science, technology and medicine that we must obtain and retain preeminence. It is for liberty, justice, safety

---

** ibid

and opportunity that all people, regardless of other differences, unite to preserve and to defend.

Human lives, worldwide, will be enriched "if" all nations could resolve to abandon warfare as an option in foreign relations? Is modern warfare actually a realistic possibility today, where no nation can be a winner? Wisdom would dictate that our nation, the most preeminent nation in the world, is in a strong position to vigorously spearhead such a proposal. A peaceful world would be the greatest national defense of all. Let us compete on the basis of culture versus culture!

Our common defense being so inextricably bound to international relations mandates some special and specific bipartisan congressional arrangements to interface with administrative arrangements in the formulation, understanding and conduct of our foreign relations. The United States should always present a unified front and purpose since this is a principle factor of our common defense. Continuity in most human endeavors is a desirable factor and it becomes a most desirous component in the field of foreign relations.

Consider the argument for this position made in the Federalist papers LXII, "to trace the mischievous effects of mutable government, would fill a volume – it forfeits the respect and confidence of other nations, (friend and foe) and advantages connected with national character. An individual, who is observed to be not constant to his plans, or perhaps to carry on his affairs without any plan at all, is marked at once by all prudent people, as a speedy victim to his own unsteadiness and folly. His more friendly neighbors may pity him, but all will decline to connect their fortunes with his. And not a few will seize the opportunity of making their fortunes out of his. One nation is to another what one individual is to another".

Can a more cogent argument be made for a bipartisan approach to foreign relations? Foreign relations are a special art and require the best intelligence and professional training we can bring to the table. Ambassadors and their staffs need to be well-versed in a nation's governmental arrangements and organization, their history, their culture, their economy, their national aspirations and their language.

All ambassadors and embassy staffs should maintain apolitical stances as professional representatives of the United States. Obviously the president must have a principle role in this bipartisan approach and just as obviously the Secretary of State must be acceptable and hold the confidence of the president. The crux of the matter is to maintain continuity in our foreign relations rather than any abrupt change except as such a change or alteration of policy is called for by changing circumstances.

Divide and conquer is a political maxim for those who are vying for advantage and power. This applies also to those external elements which pose a danger to our national solidarity and we must be alert to this stratagem through our foreign relations. There always can be differences of opinion regarding various aspects of strategy and where our priorities should be focused, however, when all available intelligence can be shared, our objectives will become more obvious and consensus will be more likely. Valid opinions on any matter or issue, requires full information documented by facts.

Our common defense requires a strong and well planned foreign relations program integrated with a comprehensive long-range strategic plan. This is another persuasive reason why our foreign relations should always be bipartisan so that the nation continues to pursue its objectives and presents a unified front. A critical part of this objective is development of a long-range, comprehensive national strategic plan addressing foreign relations, world conditions, national priorities, appropriate military preparedness, the domestic economy, national infrastructure needs, educational needs, internal security, with state and public involvement. Obviously timely updating is a prerequisite.

With expected differences between liberal and conservative persuasions on domestic issues, our nation must present a unified front to all others. To achieve this national necessity will require us to constitutionally establish a bipartisan structure for the conduct of foreign relations.

This could take the form of an ad hoc council, consisting of the Secretary of State acting as chairman, representative leadership of both political parties from the Senate and House of Representatives together with appropriate administrative advisers. Since the appointment of the Secretary of State requires senate approval there is an element of bipartisanship already in place.

Certainly the president must lead and his/her choice of Secretary of State also should lead such a bipartisan panel. Since the overall objective of our foreign relations is to protect and enhance national strategic interests there should always be common ground on which to base our foreign relations. The objective would be to develop a dependable foreign-policy which would not change every four or eight years with the election of a new president. Our foreign relations should present greater continuity and improved relations will result.

As we have seen, foreign relations are a distinct career which has major impacts on our nation. These impacts affect everyone and make no distinction along party lines. It is not an area for partisan one-upsmanship. It is an area where transitory advantages gained by a few are often a loss of liberty to many. It is an area where we must present a united front, where internal bickering has no place. Our relations with other nations should always have the objective of securing and pursuing areas of mutual benefit and interest. Dependability and continuity in our relationships with other nations are vital ingredients.

Aside from foreign relations, for optimal public protection all governmental levels must be synchronized, each contributing and pulling in the same direction – alignment of purpose. State involvement is significant to bring the full force and effect of our nation into play. Professionally managed cities, where most Americans live, are a vital ingredient. Cities require professionally trained managers just the same as giant corporations. Understanding and preparation of requirements for civilian preparedness should be a national priority. The availability and dependability of first responders is a vital factor.

The danger of internal divisiveness reflects the more imperfect side of our human disposition and becomes a sphere in our social and political arrangements which we must devise provisions to ameliorate. Traits such as arrogance, intemperance, self-seeking, intolerance, egotism, and an unenlightened disregard for the foundations of our national purpose must be exposed. The voting booth becomes a place to reject these traits. Internal erosions take the form of complacency, impregnability, self-righteousness, factionalism, demagoguery, and educational deficiency. Knowledge of the nation's history and participation of the public in governmental affairs are the requisite arenas for good citizenship. Does our common defense based upon internal solidarity fall short of what it needs to be?

The fact that most elections attract participation of less than a majority of those eligible to vote constitutes a grave warning that a vital element of our political and social order faces an imminent crisis. Public distrust, apathy, and skepticism regarding the value of their vote, disenchantment with representation and the fairness of elections constitute the major causes for the lack of citizen participation. Our public education system becomes a prime resource to instill in all children the merits and responsibilities of citizenship in a republic.

It is difficult to emphasize too strongly the critical importance of a first rate educational system which is open to all. Education is the pivotal and decisive element of a republic – our liberty and our common defense depends on it. Without a sound knowledge of one's history and how generations of Americans have made great personal sacrifices to achieve what we now possess, much of its importance and meaning is lost. For people to live in a republic and not know and understand it, how it came to be and what it depends on, defies its continuance. Our common defense is greatly strengthened by understanding our history.

Every citizen should be exposed early in life to the monumental risks and sacrifices our forebears endured in the cause of human freedom. Every citizen should know how their own government is organized, how it operates and what is required of citizenship to maintain it. In a nutshell, without a knowledgeable citizenry our experiment in democracy will gradually become feeble and will be replaced by a government which does not accept citizenship – that designation will be changed to "lower-class" and then to serfdom. This is why social stratification poses an imminent threat. Only an educated and involved citizenry will be able to maintain an enduring common defense for democracy.

Another necessity for defense is an effective government capable of and responsive to social needs and natural disasters as well as international circumstances. Astute leadership in any undertaking, public or private, is essential for success. Our common defense must acknowledge the necessity for protecting our environment in order to maintain healthy and desirable living conditions. It also includes taking official notice and action regarding global warming. Our nation today emits more greenhouse gases than any other nation in the world and more than the combined releases of several other nations including China and Europe.

The effects of global warming occur in a variety of ways, some areas receive greater precipitation than usual while others receive less; some are hotter and some are cooler. Storms are more frequent in number and in intensity. Habitats of both flora and fauna are beginning to change which poses a threat to both. Sea levels are already reflecting the melting ice caps at both poles as well as glaciers around the world.

Greenland's ice cap has been receding at a rapid rate resulting in the need to redraw the boundaries of that country. The total loss of that ice cap will raise the ocean levels by some 20 feet endangering coastal areas as well as several islands in the Pacific. Perhaps of greater dread in the near-term, could be the frozen peat bogs of Siberia, which if melted would release billions of tons of greenhouse gases acting to raise temperatures even more quickly.

The signs, verified by scientists and researchers around the world, are too real to be ignored. To be belittled or pushed aside due to demagogic political reasons is folly to the extreme. Although there may be some question as to all of the contributing factors there is no reasonable or logical question that the influences of mankind are a significant influence. But regardless of reasons the threat is catastrophic and requires national as well as worldwide attention and cooperation to exert the best efforts to control the situation as best we can.

It has been long proven in many fields that there is a limit to all things and in the ability of our planet to cope with an ever increasing population and the unwise use of nature's bounty is no exception. "The uncomfortable truth is that the current scale and character of human activities are decreasing the planet's life support capacity."[***]

A total approach to our common defense implies protecting representative government also as well as a defense against foreign threats. Obviously it is our republic for which defense is required. To do this more explicit constitutional guarantees need to be instituted to deny all devious devices and subversive arrangements which tend to limit, restrict, confuse, intimidate or inconvenience otherwise willing and eligible voters. Elections of federal officeholders should be controlled by federal statutes requiring bipartisan arrangements open to complete public review. Public confidence in the electoral process is fundamental to the democratic process. The right to vote is a constituent part of freedom of speech. Fundamental national guarantees which protect individual and human rights also become guarantees for our common defense.

Speakers at various celebrations commemorating our nation's success and merits habitually refer to the greatness of the American people and how Americans can do anything and overcome any obstacle. These are things we like to hear and who doesn't accept praise? But when we accept these accolades and feel that burst of pride do we also include ourselves or do we stop to consider what our contributions have been? Does the truth tell us that for the most part, what we enjoy and rely on are conditions and circumstances which past generations produced or made possible? Have we, in our time, improved our society? Have we corrected the flaws that time, politics and practice have revealed? Or has our political system tended to discourage the typical American? Public confidence in our governmental system is essential and every reasonable

---

[***] Understanding Social Problems, fifth addition, Linda Mooney, David Knox and Carolyn Schacht

effort needs to be made to restore it. How have we participated in our common defense?

There should be little question that in today's world every effort should be made to counter any nation's military strength. But there are at least three major aspects that must be carefully monitored. First, in our efforts to maintain maximum military strength we must carefully guard against military inroads into national policy. Civilian control through duly elected and publicly responsible representatives must always be maintained.

Let us heed President Dwight Eisenhower's comments in 1961, "in the councils of government we must guard against the acquisition of unwarranted influence, whether sought or unsought, by the military-industrial complex. The potential for the disastrous rise of misplaced power exists and will continue to persist". The general had just witnessed the results of such an alliance in Europe and Japan where the military-industrial complex dominated national policy.

If we have overextended ourselves in wars and foreign "police actions" the responsibility, accountability and fault should be placed only secondarily on the Pentagon. The finger must be pointed first toward Congress and the executive branches for the policies and actions requiring the level and type of military involvement necessary which our best foreign relations policies indicate. The Pentagon does what it is designed to do. Next, a great deal of fault lies with control and oversight of Pentagon activities – their priorities and our national strategic plan used to establish and direct them. This is the essence of the danger President Eisenhower inferred.

Secondly, there will be always a debate concerning how much of the nation's resources should be devoted to military power. We now spend more than China, Russia, Britain and France combined. To emphasize the obvious, our resources are not unlimited. A vital public question is how the expense burden will be distributed. Hopefully, such a burden will be shared as it was in World War II. Giant international corporations may not be so willing to share this burden as a result of some divided loyalties unless they are profiting in the process. This is especially true of those corporations where the state funds of other nations have invested heavily in their stock. Serious debates can occur as to how the available resources are distributed among the military establishment. There will be always the problem of how we attend to other national requirements such as our aging infrastructure, schools, the national power grid and vital social needs. The public coffers never have enough to meet and satisfy all competing demands.

The third major aspect has to do with long-range strategic planning. Much effort has been made along these lines but more emphasis needs to be made on total and comprehensive involvement including the role of cities and states, strengthening of international ties and commitments and all-out efforts in the field of cyber technology. Here again the question and problem of federalism raises its head.

Our complete national strength can only be realized if there is true alignment of purpose and effort through all levels of government: nation, state, county and city. For the sake of our existence in the modern world we must constitutionally allow – we must insist – that there be alignment of national policy concerning our common defense efforts throughout our governmental structure. When our national interests are directed along a specific course and several states ignore it or pursue programs which are contrary to it, our national strength is weakened. From the top to the bottom of our governmental structures we must stand united; once again alignment of purpose is critical.

In regard to local government, cities can play an important role. In particular their police and fire operations, their public works operations and their building codes are fundamental to public safety and to recovery from hurricanes, tornadoes, earthquakes or terrorist attack. If these functions are fully supported and managed a very strong and vital part of our common defense will be in place.

When we speak of Americans we should be mindful of the fact that we are an amalgamation of every ethnic group in the world, it is not an ethnic appellation but rather a designation for a new breed of people who have created the world's greatest democracy. In a sense the only true Americans are the American Indians. As we take pride in being today's Americans let us be thankful that our fathers and mothers or grandparents or our great-great grandparents had the fortitude, necessity, dream or aspiration to travel to a new far-off land that welcomed all "who yearned to be free." Our land should always be open to those who legally seek this land of opportunity. This is how our nation became stronger, improved our republic and our common defense.

To a substantial degree, "we", the present generation of adult age, have prospered due to the educational system, the technological advances and the infrastructure improvements instituted by those who came before us. We are not the creators of this largesse but the benefactors. It was the foundation that our forebears built and the bounty they left to us that made the United States the world's most powerful nation.

Now, as we proceed further into the 21st century, what will we do to improve society, our educational system and our political system which are all ingredients of our common defense? What we do in our time will have many repercussions, favorable or unfavorable, for many decades to come.

None of the foregoing is intended to downgrade recent and contemporary accomplishments in several fields of endeavor. Some have advanced social welfare. This is particularly true in the fields of medicine, science and technology. It is our governance and social mores that are timely and critical to address. They are relevant to our common defense and emphasize the role which individual citizens play in society. The attitude and involvement of citizens is a highly important ingredient which determines how a nation is governed. The importance which society places on individual schooling and responsibility will predict the effectiveness and direction of our social solidarity and the political and socioeconomic spheres as well as our strength as a nation.

Our common defense depends upon a totality of factors which constitutes us as a nation. It depends upon our defending the values and goals expressed in the preamble of our Constitution. It depends on an effective government, an ethical and responsive society, a productive economic system, a true justice system and a universal educational system. All of these are vital to ensure our common defense and thus our survival as the world's greatest example of democracy.

Even a casual perusal of these factors demonstrates clearly that the bar set forth in our founding values and the goals enunciated in the constitution's preamble were extremely high. Those goals and values are so high indeed that we are finding them difficult not only to achieve but to maintain. But here-in lies the key to the greatness of a nation's people – achievement of low goals can never represent greatness. It is the constant, never-ending search to reach lofty goals which has and can continue to make this nation strong and great.

In general terms our form of governance and way of life will represent what the vast majority of people want and will accept. Essentially all people want the same things. When the question turns to how these things are to be realized we are met with many different views. This dilemma becomes more evident by the total transformation of our nation from 13 largely congruous states situated along the Atlantic coast to 50 heterogeneous states spanning the continent and separated by an ocean.

Our differences consist of most of the disparities found in the cultures and religions known to humankind. Conversely our cohesion springs from the human bond relating to liberty, security, and democratic governance which are the constituent elements worth working and fighting for. Although expressed in many ways religion, in some form has played a prominent role in our national way of life and contributes to the determination of our people and our common defense.

The difficulties we face to improve our governance and to maintain internal cohesion on which our common defense depends are exacerbated by numerous factors. Among these are a disinterested electorate, an inferior educational system, the rise of single issue and ideological zealots, a flawed system for electing our representatives, and the growing gap between necessary requirements for democratic governance and the institutional powers and influence of multinational corporations.

The fundamental problem of this last named factor is how we relate to the goals of democracy with institutions which depend upon and serve several nations. For democracy to survive, first and foremost, there must be concordance between the government and its economy which recognizes and protects the interests and welfare of the people. For a nation to be safe and secure, its economy, just as its citizens, must be willing to give total support and allegiance.

This sampling of today's complexities exposes the insufficiency of thinking that the world's best military is all that is needed to provide for our common defense. It reveals decidedly how vital it is to defend, enhance and preserve our core values as expressed by the preamble of our constitution.

These core values translate into the necessity for fair and ethical practices in social, economic and political affairs. These values should dispel the acceptance of practices of hatred or expressed contempt for any others unlike ourselves or to allow favorable exceptions to anyone regarding general public requirements. The real bond for everyone is allegiance to the constitution – the blueprint for a republic.

"Out of many we are one" expresses an indispensable requirement that we – all us – are bound together in the cause of liberty and representative government. It demonstrates our need to depend upon one another for our common good and our common defense. Our common defense hinges upon the preservation and improvement of our internal solidarity, our dedication, first and foremost, to freedom and justice for all. It was James Madison who told us that "equal laws protecting rights....the best guarantee of loyalty and love of country." Otherwise we will be witness to self-seeking, demagoguery, avarice and complacency ruling our tomorrows.

"The United States is the only advanced society in which productivity has been steadily rising over the past two decades while the incomes of the majority – eight out of ten – have stagnated or fallen. …. In the face of numerous recessions, median family income had been declining since the 1970s; the 1990s were remarkable in that the expanding economy had virtually no impact on the poor or on working-class incomes." The GINI Index, a measure of inequality reported by the United States Census Bureau.

Social Problems, Robert Hienes, third edition 2010

"The Luxembourg Income Status, comparing the United States with many other industrialized nations, found that the rich in the United States had more disposable income (between one quarter and one half more) than the rich in any of the other nations studied and the poor in the United States had the least disposable income, suggesting that the rich in the United States are better off than the rich in most of the industrialized nations and poor are among the poorest in the industrialized world".

The Social Health of the Nations, Miringolf and Miringolf

CHAPTER 6

Promote The General Welfare

"We would like to see an America where the welfare of every citizen is the concern of all, which makes full use of its great capacities to advance the welfare of all – not a welfare state – but a state with meaningful compassion for those whose welfare has been undermined." John F. Kennedy, speech in Chicago, 1961

If the United States is worth saving it has to be for a government which will promote the general welfare. When the constitutional framers set forth their purposes of this new nation a constituent part ordained was to do just that, promote the general welfare! Why is this fundamental for a democratic society? Their intent was to establish a direction and a purpose for the new republic to achieve universal opportunity and security for everyone – the basic physical and material well-being of its people. This was a completely contrary notion about governmental rule of that day. From today's standpoint what good is a nation that doesn't promote the general welfare? The "American dream" has become the chief result of that promotion of the general welfare.

This unique and new concept for a government to be formulated with an avowed purpose of promoting the general welfare of its people soon caught the eye of people around the world. Oligarchies and monarchies and other totalitarian forms of government existed only for the benefit of the ruling class while extracting all they could from the "commoners". In these regimes a person's place in the social order depended entirely on who their parents were. No government before 1789 recognized the dignity of the individual or set forth a written Constitution documenting a method to achieve it. Societal control had existed always to benefit only those who held power by the force of arms and, at times, aided by religion.

In these earlier monarchies, ruled through the divine right of Kings, the division of society into classes was the established norm. The upper-class ruled and claimed the benefits and wealth of the kingdom. The King's military received special favors as well. Those relative few who served the upper-class and the military existed as a somewhat "middle-class". The masses of people were serfs or commoners who lived only to serve the King. Throughout history where societies formed into distinct classes, the promotion of the general welfare was not considered since it would be contrary to class distinctions. Throughout history class distinction has always been a matter of wealth and/or governmental and military position. Judging the United States as a model, is there any hint of such a division in society emerging?

Our constitutional framers knew that the constitution they proposed could not provide for every eventuality which the nation would be called upon to handle. Times have borne them out. Common sense tells us that our founding fathers also reasoned that future generations would exercise their intelligence to make the necessary corrections to preserve and enhance what they had been given. Article V of our constitution provides us with two methods to make the changes we deem necessary and desirable. It has already been used 27 times.

Like all objectives of a true republic – equality under law, opportunity, justice, and representation – none are achieved unless all features of the democratic machinery are effectively in place and operating according to their purpose. This will be an aspiration which will be always a work in progress and very difficult to attain. But the difficulties to achieve our objective of a valid republic do not translate into impossibility and should never be an excuse for not exercising our best efforts to institute improvements in our governance. Constitutional amendments can be very difficult, but for us, not as difficult as losing a republic.

The idea of the American dream is an enduring goal for everyone to seek and should be earmarked as a fundamental right. Everyone should have an equal access to education, healthcare, safe and secure neighborhoods and an equal opportunity for any legitimate goal which their honest and competent efforts can attain. Justice and equality under law must not depend upon access to the foremost legal firms or to a person's public persona.

The "American dream" essentially encompasses the kind of life which is desired by all human beings. Our forefathers directed that this would be a nation that promoted the equality of mankind and those inalienable rights to life, liberty and the pursuit of happiness. They advanced the idea that collectively we could accomplish great things which could not be achieved otherwise. Every true American has believed they were right!

In a century and a half this fledgling nation rose to the pinnacle of the world's powers. But having achieved that lofty position what are the results? Have we made life easier for everyone? Are governmental, social and economic systems in harmony with this dictum of the United States Constitution and Declaration of Independence? When some 46 million people (2011) live in poverty, when nearly 15% of American households experience low or very low food security,[U. S. Department of Agriculture] can the American dream ever be but a dream for them? (The poverty level is designated for a family of four with an annual income below $23,021 per year.)

What we desperately need to do is guard against a situation where education becomes unaffordable or unattainable. There is a close correlation between the number of uneducated people and the poverty level in society. Aproximately 8.2% of those without a high school education are among the unemployed. As the education level increases, those with a college education show less than 2.5% unemployment. The more desperate people become the lower the market price is for their labor. In such circumstances society takes on the same appearance as the old monarchies of the middle ages. Currently total income of wage earners equals the smallest share of the national income since 1929 – the start of the Great Depression.

Educated workers require higher wages for their services. Laws protecting reasonable and socially acceptable workers' rights and working conditions will show favorable societal results. As workers are able to receive larger incomes on a national basis, consumer spending will rise and businesses will profit. An equitable balance between labor and management will vary in every business and only can be achieved when fair-minded people are determined to work in the interests of all concerned including the effects on and interests of society.

As more and more people acquire income in excess of their normal living requirements, many new avenues for spending are opened to them. From a societal point of view this can pose some potential dangers. This is where the subject of our social mores must be addressed. Expenditures for harmful habits, frivolous and unproductive activities represent a profligate lifestyle – which may continue for one or two generations. On the other hand if this excess income is spent for meaningful vocations, remodeling or purchasing new homes, higher education or gaining extra skills, and developing a family savings, it develops ingredients to advance society and the general welfare of the nation.

All of us use and need leisure time and we will spend $100 or $200 or more to see men run up and down a gridiron, or others running to put a ball through a hoop, or others skating on ice to slam the puck into a net, or others on a grassy field to kick a ball into a net and, hopefully, we will enjoy the event. We may also enjoy some ballpark franks or go to a restaurant afterwards – busy, working people need some diversion and relaxation time. But, consider the reverse side, and see how many will vote to raise their taxes by $100 or $200 a year to improve our schools, repair or build a new bridge – or will the odds for approval be improved if the ballot question was to build a new sports arena where "private" interests stand to make millions of dollars at public expense! It becomes a question of where the public's values and priorities are tested. The kind of values we truly follow and firmly support will predict what our lives will be like and what our country will be like – they define the American culture.

In a republic should there be legal guarantees concerning human rights applicable to the work place? Should our economy perform in harmony and be compatible with democracy? Such a concept should not question requirements for appropriate work rules, supervisorial prerogatives and management direction. It is the dignity of humanity, the social and economic impacts which are vital principles in a republic, and must be observed.

We should never be deluded in thinking that any public enterprise [or human institution] does not require rules and oversight to the degree necessary to protect the public welfare. We should not have to be reminded of the frailties of our species. In his farewell address in 1796, President George Washington stated "few men have the virtue enough to withstand the highest bidder". Consider what people will do for money and consider that numerous multinational corporations net tens of billions of dollars annually and one will realize the challenge it poses to the people's government as to who shall rule over society. Only in a true republic with representatives who are held by constitutional requirements to be beholden only to the public, can our society withstand the power and financial strength posed by these multinational corporations.

To invigorate and promote the general welfare suggests that an equal opportunity to earn and develop reasonable wealth is a basic component of the American dream. Without question there will be many different concepts of what constitutes a sufficiency of wealth. The point however, in viewing society as a whole, is whether our socioeconomic and political systems provide everyone with an equal opportunity to fulfill their aspirations according to their abilities and qualifications. Everyone will not achieve that highest pinnacle – many will not want it! But failure to do so should not result from reasons stemming from social status, ethnicity, gender or economic and educational restraints or from political forces or arrangements.

IS THE UNITED STATES WORTH SAVING?

Historically, nations have pursued many different forms of economic enterprise. None have been totally successful. A free, competitive market system has yielded the best results but faces many problems with the emergence of globalized economies. Competition takes on different dimensions becoming totally dependent on the cheapest labor, meager or nonexistent regulations on hazardous materials and advertising. These circumstances encompassing globalized economies supersede individual rights – they always have! Aside from lower prices and some inferior products, another result is that some have contained hazardous substances while others have posed safety risks, having been banned in the U.S.A. for many years. Is it in our national interest to allow such practices for lower prices? Trade agreements should seek worker standards and timetables for greater parity in monetary values and import export equalization.

Such conditions as these do not represent the kind of capitalism which should have evolved from laissez-faire concepts which never advocated child labor, starvation wages, 16 hour and seven-day work weeks. This type of enterprise is akin to slavery and those who profit from it, by comparison, have only a foreign nation to distinguish them from slaveholders before the American Civil War. This refers to the form of enterprise permitted in China and other nations to develop an enormously favorable balance of trade of exports over imports. It is basically a modern form of 17th and 18th century mercantilism, a policy which Adam Smith totally rejected. The enormous profits from this practice are placed in state funds which can be invested in the stock of multinational corporations which generate additional profits which are returned to the originating state funds.

There appears to be some confusion in the public mind revealing numerous interpretations of capitalism. Some seem to associate capitalism only with that bygone day of Adam Smith and his concept of laissez faire national economic policy. His reasoning was a perfect fit for the 18th century circumstances when business enterprise was small, served limited geographical areas and where the artisans were personally known by most of the consuming public which they served. It was a time when few chemicals, if any, were known or used, where the public water supply and the air around them were unaffected and the character and reputation of the craftsmen was public knowledge. Promoting and protecting public welfare has taken on a completely new and expanded meaning and challenge as well as has free, competitive enterprise which now faces a worldwide economy. Today, only small business seems to fit the concepts of open, free and competitive enterprise.

Many readers today would be surprised that Adam Smith also condemned advertising since it interfered with free competition and therefore the general welfare. In today's business world advertising has become a leading factor in competition. Every thoughtful person is aware of the misleading, false and exaggerated advertisements and yet they are successful. In a republic, the people's government should provide reasonable protection to require fundamentally accurate and truthful advertising. Giant corporations, mostly global enterprises, pose an entirely different social, governmental and economic consideration on how business is controlled and how we protect our representative system and promote the general welfare.

Job security in today's global economy has been the greatest problem for the American worker. The accompanying result has been a loss of income which has been declining or stagnant for decades. The popular corporate explanation and strategy, in order to compete, is to be able to alter operations on short notice, that is, be highly flexible. This flexibility results in low job security for the worker when various parts – or all – of a business is outsourced. There is no longer a "social contract" between corporations and their employees. Profit is the only criterion to remain a viable business. This factor also necessitates advertising to reach consumers by any means that will attract a large audience. Thus, advertising becomes a foremost element of competition for business success. This circumstance reveals how an unsuspecting public requires some protection.

In today's world many thousands of typical citizens own stock in various private enterprises. It is in this realm where more public protection may be required. Numerous questions arise as to whether investors and stockholders receive appropriate consideration in corporate decisions. This question becomes relative to whether economic practices are compatible with republican principles. How democratic should corporations become when doing business in a republic? Are corporate rules which allow management and boards of directors to make all financial decisions without stockholder approval a reasonable practice?

A case in point is whether the exorbitant compensation levels of many hundreds of CEOs and other top management personnel are necessary, advisable or in the best interests of the business? Do millions of dollars spent on political campaigns serve the best interests of all stockholders? Should stockholders have a say in such matters? Would it be reasonable to require that all management personnel as well as the boards of directors be stockholders in the corporation? From a purely governmental standpoint what should be assured in a republic is, first, investors should be recognized appropriately in their company's operations and, second, the safety and authenticity of all products and services should never infringe on or endanger public welfare, health or safety.

Other views of capitalism are to allow any entrepreneur to operate without any or, at least, only a few regulations. This concept would be appropriate if all people were totally honest and fair, gave total attention to preventing harmful public effects, provided fair compensation and working conditions, respected the environment and refused government subsidies and tax breaks. The undeniable truth is that when operating decisions boil down to profits, profits come in first every time. It is obvious that every successful business must make a profit which is the only reason to risk capital and effort. The fine line that society must follow is to protect public health, safety and welfare while permitting beneficial and required enterprise. Among the tenets of our social value system is the requirement that protection of the public welfare must predominate.

Pause to consider what public value the economy is if it does not elevate the human condition and way of life! The American dream consists of achieving security, a home, good health, sufficient leisure time, a meaningful vocation and a nest egg for older age. To make a living in order to achieve these requirements becomes a means to an end and not the end in itself. The economy does not become a way of life, it is a function in life; it is a variation in today's world, comparable to hunting and gathering in ancient times. The purpose of the economy is to support society so that it flourishes and enhances people's lives.

In order to understand the situation one must look at the historical record and review sagas of the tobacco companies, chemical companies, mining companies, railroads, drug companies, financial institutions, and the list goes on. Just where does the public welfare fit in and who is it that must protect the public's rights and welfare? Once again, as always, the general public welfare requires necessary and reasonable protection – that is a fundamental purpose and reason we have a republic!

Drawing on personal experience I recall the passage of the original Clean Water Act. The basic requirement of the law prohibited any discharge of effluent into any river which made the river more contaminated. This required thousands of cities, which pursued such a practice, to construct treatment facilities.

Our city, incorporated in the mid-1800s, still utilized a combined storm water and sewer system. This meant constructing in every street new sewer mains and storm drains, more than a hundred miles, and this, in turn, required every house and habitable dwelling or building, to be connected. This was a seven years project and a great expense to be paid off over some 3 decades.

As other upstream cities cleaned up their discharges [the law applied to corporations as well] every city downstream had to periodically improve their treatment processes. The result, after several years, was clean water in American rivers and streams.

In recent years some very sad and startling news was reported. Today, once again, many of our rivers and streams are heavily polluted! Not so much with sewage today but with all types of chemicals and industrial waste. It seems that many corporations, somehow, have gotten exemptions which cities, our people, have neither requested nor received.

One can only conjecture how this has occurred, but perhaps, only one attempt at an answer will be enough.

It is policies, regulatory lapses and legal loopholes which allow corporate polluters free access to our nation's natural resources – water, air and pristine habitats – that degrade the environment but also endangers the world climate. Today there are nearly 2 dozen states reporting pollution in their rivers ranging from Maine and Vermont to Ohio and Michigan and to Montana and Washington. Our nation now releases one-fourth of the worldwide total of global warming gases annually although our population is less than 5% of the world population. This is a prime example of how short term gains predict major problems in our future.

When the Clear Skies Initiative was repealed in the early 2000s it deleted health protections prescribed under the Federal Clean Air Act. This permitted electric utility companies to discharge untreated contaminants into the air. Only one state, California, overturned this provision having battled smog problems for many years. Certain pollutions such as mercury and asthma provoking ozone particulates coming from coal burning power plants were also excused from requirements of the Federal Clean Air Act. From a public point of view the problem was compounded by the repeal of the "polluter-pays-tax" – a fund which had been used to clean up toxic spills and dumps used for waste. This is now a public expense and illustrates how loopholes in public laws transfer a business expense to the taxpayer. This is another example for the need of a social conscience in all business undertakings and how the public interest is served, or not served.

When we witnessed the outsourcing of manufacturing, as well as the previously recited situation, we must look at business realistically. No business can exist without profits and profits are the principal force which drives entrepreneurs. This is the obvious reason why businesses seek access to the least costly labor market available. If a business can produce their product cheaper by using child labor, can require workdays of 12 to 14 hours and six or seven days a week, pay little or nothing for healthcare, injuries, vacations or retirement and have no government regulation – except, perhaps some consideration to key government figures – the business decision becomes clear. These facts do not make the situation right but they may become the difference between making enormous profits and even staying in business.

Realistically the consuming public must rely upon governmental scrutiny to protect health and safety concerns. Until such time when trade and monetary practices are equalized we are not apt to see any great change. As third world nations become wealthier and their people demand their basic human rights perhaps we will see another evolution in economic practices. Our definition of capitalism must continue to insist on responsible competitive enterprise – it is not realistic to expect worldwide living standards to rise to near equality in less than three or four decades, if ever.

The general welfare for virtually everyone requires that life's necessities plus a reasonable amount of disposable income is available to them. No one could deny that food, clothing, comfortable shelter, health protection and reasonable leisure time are basic to human happiness. These necessities, along with an equitable savings for protection during older years, are enough to enjoy the blessings of life and liberty – that is, for most people.

Many will strive for an even higher standard and there should be room always for some greater luxuries. But more of all of these things may never be enough for some people and a reasonable egalitarian society is most likely unattainable given today's societal norms. However, to strive for a better society is a component part of the pursuit of happiness and worthy of our best efforts to achieve. Our goals and objectives, looking to the future, need to continue the pursuit toward an ever improving republic – one step at a time.

A few people will always want more, much more even to obsession. Unfortunately greed and avarice of a few have always plagued society. The dilemma arises as to how a fair and just society can accommodate those of such obdurate compulsions. Self-interest and a desire for better things are natural and a necessary factor in human progress. But exaggerated concepts of self-worth and narcissism result in antisocial behavior and becomes a hindrance in a free society. In some instances such practices can and do demean others. Those who persist in such behavior should be controlled by appropriate legal methods including taxation.

Promoting the general welfare, which can change over time, requires a well thought-out public policy. It requires awareness of and attention to what we perceive as the bad side of human nature. Wisdom would dictate that the public should exercise reasonable controls relating to worker safety, hours of work, a livable wage, healthcare and retirement benefits. Many business practices have shown a social conscience but at the same time the reverse has been the case. It is the impact upon society which must guide governmental practice.

The distribution of gains from any enterprise should be performed on an equitable basis and certainly, risk, ideas, hard work, and yes, maybe some sleepless nights, should be amply rewarded. But as in all things there are limits and the consumer and society as a whole must be considered in the equation. Considering that the essential objective of commercial endeavors must be a profit, what is best for the people or even what is actually needed becomes secondary objectives. This is why advertising becomes paramount in the process. Every enterprise depends upon the society which it serves. None could exist and prosper without public streets and highways, public police and fire protection, water supply and the public amenities which provide their workforce and a population of consumers.

As to what should be the spread between the total benefits of the lowest full-time worker compared to that of the highest-paid executive, there is sure to be many different views. What we know is that our nation faired very well when the average differential was approximately $1-$35 during the middle of the 20th century, our so-called Golden Age. Today the differential is approximately $1-$343. Could something more like $1-$75 or $150 be a more reasonable spread? What is reasonable and fair will vary with the enterprise as well as a person's socioeconomic outlook and social conscience. No two business enterprises are the same and no single solution will suffice for all situations, it is the overall average among all businesses which most directly affect society and the national welfare.

Whatever it may be will be substantially determined by market conditions which are primarily affected and an area of ongoing conjecture for sociologists and economists. What is certain is that our economy goes through periodic boom and bust cycles. We know that tax policies and Federal Reserve decisions are significant factors. Also we know that the percentage of national income received by the wealthiest 10% in 1928, the eve of the great depression, was virtually identical to that of 2007 when less than 10% of the people received almost half of the national income. Is this an anomaly or is it indicative of a mal-distribution of income affecting consumerism and therefore the national economy?

How citizens should pay their fair share of taxes is always a subject which elicits many viewpoints. Regardless of the viewpoint, statistics may be enlightening in connection with economic business cycles. During the boom years in the mid-1950s, the highest tax rate was 91%. The wealthiest 10% of Americans in 1953 received 32.3% of the national income. In 1962 the top income tax rate was 77%. It was still 70% in 1972 and has gone down to 35% at this writing, the lowest rate for nearly a century. [The 16th amendment in 1913, provided for the income tax. It provided major funding for World War I]

Notwithstanding a 35% income tax rate applicable to the wealthiest 2%, they pay, on an average, only 19% thanks to a tax code provision allowing a 15% rate on capital gains and dividends. Curiously this provision means that if you work for a wage or salary you will pay, on average, 8% to 12% more than money earns on its own – capital gains. Do tax requirements of this type meet the test of equal protection of the laws? Loopholes in the tax code are not put there by the public – they are put there as a result of the influence on "our" legislators. Obviously they benefit only a few and do not meet the test of equal protection of the laws.

It is the boom and bust cycles of our economy which degrades society and the public should keep in mind the economic truism that a mal-distribution of wealth results in reduced consumerism which causes everyone to suffer – manufacturer, distributor, salesman and the public at large. Economic policy should always endeavor to see that all reasonable efforts are made to maintain a balance in the nation's economic engines. This is an area of economics where top economists differ widely. The relationship between the Federal Reserve Board, the president and the people's representatives and the influence of Wall Street has spurred heated debate since the Great Depression of the 1930s. As in all matters answers exist which a true representative government should seek.

In effect we have two capitals, Washington DC and Wall Street. They are two different sources of power in our society – the people's government and money. There are many common grounds for the two but there are often fundamental differences which arise regarding basic issues of the country's economy. The reason for this is somewhat obvious: first, they serve two diverse masters and second, they do not fully understand or accept the other's objectives. These objectives diverge in two principal areas; one concerns how and for what money is to be used while the other must determine how the public welfare and interests are to be served. These seemingly, are two inextricably opposite agendas which must be reconciled for our nation to prosper and progress.

What magnitude of difference in terms of wealth and the quality of living standards should the obvious variations in the human condition be considered as acceptable from the standpoint of the general welfare? Are such variations inevitable in human society? Can we continue to say that we believe in democracy and at the same time permit unlimited discrepancies to exist? To what degree can we accept these disparities and not create thereby a class-based society? What degree of change would occur in such situations if education, health care, satisfactory living environments and opportunity were equally open to everyone? Would the availability and provision for these constituent components which effect human advancement, be a reasonable policy objective to follow in order to promote the general welfare? Only through open public discussion and debate among well-meaning and informed citizens can we arrive at some reasonable conclusions. For the sake of preserving and enhancing public welfare such decisions must take place and it is the responsibility of the people's representatives to bring it about.

Our nation, the shining beacon for freedom and individual liberty on earth, attained this distinction by being able to work for the ideals expressed in the Constitution, through example, by universal education, by invention, and by free competitive enterprise. There have been contributions by people of every race and creed – all seeking their version of that "American dream". All of this is a result of our founding values and an outgrowth of promotion of the general welfare. These constitute a formula which we should strive to continue in order to improve and prosper.

There is no questioning the great differences in human conditions in our country. We must recognize that there are many reasons which cause and contribute to this predicament. Factors including prenatal care, very early and free schooling, parenting and family life, ongoing healthcare, neighborhood environment and exposure to lifestyles are among the many components which differentiate us. The causes are many. Human aptitudes, intelligence, motivation, personal values and determination can vary to considerable degrees. Opportunity, timing, location, academic and vocational education, inheritance, acquaintances as well as personality enter the equation. Other factors such as personal appearance, injuries, handicaps and individual preferences also play a role. Even personal attitudes, ego, and blind luck can and do play a relevant part in the success and/or failure of many people. With all these variables it is easy to see why major disparities exist. Is it possible for social policies, over time, to minimize the adverse effects of these variables? Continued advances in medical and biological sciences may, someday, provide some answers.

The basic question becomes to what magnitude of difference in terms of wealth should such variations in human traits and conditions be acceptable to continue and still subscribe to the notion that "all men are created equal"? And to what extent does our belief in democracy allow these inevitable differences in people to separate and divide us into a class differentiated society? What are the responsibilities of the highly successful to society in a democracy? Do they depend upon society or does society depend upon them? Does the counsel of "to whom much is given, much is expected" apply? These are some of the questions which well-informed and well-meaning citizens need to debate and provide information to the public representatives in order to arrive at some social improvements. This represents a continuing quest which must continue if social and individual welfare is to be improved. Meaningful improvements can't be expected to "just happen". The use of whatever intellectual ability we possess must be applied to our governance and to our social mores.

The differences found in humanity likely will be always with us. What we can do is provide the means to lessen the most egregious situations and to require that, from a legal point of view, everyone is equal. Through conscious efforts, utilizing our best national talent to present ideas for social advancement, could practical steps be taken to improve society? Over time, possibly two or three generations, would we begin to realize a more enjoyable society in a truer republic? It is equally obvious that we have the means to alleviate the most flagrant problems. All society will benefit if we do. But do we have the resolve?

In a democracy it would seem that there should be at least the assurance that an equal opportunity to succeed be available to all. Recognition must be made to the fact that personal preferences regarding professions and careers, as well as the public importance attached to various careers, has a great bearing upon the acquisition of wealth. Should our social mores continue to consider wealth as the pinnacle of human achievement? Should our love of money be the driving force in our lives and does that equate to human happiness? Is the quest to amass great wealth a true basis to promote the general welfare? Many provocative questions, such as these, face us and they are met by ignoring them because satisfactory answers are either unavailable or they are too unpopular to face.

Our laws governing taxation currently have been filled with all sorts of tax dodges and loopholes which are not really appropriate for use by the great body of citizens. This, in turn, has been instrumental in the accumulation of wealth with no real contributions to national welfare resulting from such practices. How can this situation be equal protection of the laws or be compatible with republican principles? How does such a situation develop and why has it persisted? Is it possible that moneyed interests have been able to get "our" representatives to assist them with this special favor? A true representative government must be the source and focal point to address these situations to protect the public welfare.

It is obvious that the role of a society's value system is an extremely important factor in how business practices are accepted. In our society a consequentially determining factor has been advertising and promotion, neither of which has had a great positive effect on social values nor have they coincided with value and quality. We must seriously ask ourselves what actually contributes to society and to the human condition and place more emphasis on what will promote the general welfare. The point is to mobilize and thereby utilize the intellectual talent of our nation – let the public hear and benefit from their knowledge.

As long as the general public remains uninformed or oblivious regarding these abuses, they will continue. This is an area in which a good educational system can make strides to correct and a truly representative national government can resolve. A great source of power and strength in our nation, which is woefully underused, is located in our colleges and universities and in a few private organizations. We need to very seriously consider and develop ways to utilize these resources for the benefit of the public welfare. Congress needs their help!

A society's value system should address both personal and public well-being. Both parenting and our educational system play key roles in this matter. How Americans spend their money and their time reflects directly on the value system. Do we spend more money on entertainment than we do on education? Significant changes in this area will undoubtedly take time and over time yield great rewards. A well thought out program, compatible with the ideals of our republic and capable of promoting the general welfare, should be developed and advanced through the educational system.

IS THE UNITED STATES WORTH SAVING?

Historical facts reveal to us that we have not always been right or fair. Some of our forebears were guilty of some egregious acts. Some practices in our free enterprise system often failed the tests of honesty and fairness and our founding ideals have not always been adhered to in practice. Not all endeavors have served lofty goals and advanced the public welfare. Too often we have witnessed the less praiseworthy side of humanity such as greed, avarice, and narcissism invade industry, government and essentially all social areas. The more praiseworthy side of humanity many times has come to the rescue and either exposed or corrected some of the worst abuses. But a great deal remains to be done and public awareness will play a major role to achieve long-term results.

The struggle goes on and it clearly tells us that we must erect every reasonable barrier, provide every reasonable incentive and install new procedures, policies and strategies for government, industry, business and society in general, to align our total efforts toward promotion of the general welfare. The foregoing could serve as a master plan for an annual conference of the nation's foremost intellectuals in several fields to assess and put forth new ideas for public debate to augment our promotion of the general welfare and speed us on our path to that objective.

We must keep in mind that all of our institutions must rely on the human qualities which control them. In so doing we must be mindful that "the basic qualities of human nature persist through the ages and in part shape the societies in which we live, as they did for the ancients .... The disciplines of intellect and rationality must prevail to control primitive socially obstructive drives, which are a natural component of the human psyche. Perverted ambitions have plagued society since antiquity, from the emperors of ancient Rome to notorious leaders of modern era nations."*

Fortunately, for us, our forefathers developed a document through which the better side of our human nature is enabled to continue making strides towards a better tomorrow. No one has ever claimed that

---

* Cosmic Legacy, Greg F. Reinking quoting H.G. Wells in "Things to Come"

the realization of a true democracy would be easily accomplished. Many everyday practices and common activities play a part with some being harmonious and others discordant to the advancement of a democratic society. All the factors which collectively affect the mores of our society: personal character and behavior, family, vocations, avocations, ethics, religion, pastimes, social beliefs, educational values etc. play a role and must be addressed and directed into compatibility with the values expressed in our Declaration of Independence and the preamble of our Constitution. These, and other factors, point to the type of culture which needs to be promoted in order to build a better tomorrow.

Our nation has proven to be a melting pot for people of the world and our experience to date has shown that the general welfare is served when people are working together cooperatively. It is obvious that political divisiveness destroys national cohesion and public confidence when the various elements of the whole are going in different directions. With the exception of our military and a few dedicated public officials and individual citizens only a relative few have truly made meaningful sacrifices for this nation. Most of us have just enjoyed what we have been given without too much thought or effort about giving back to society. This perhaps is truer today than ever before when a very low percentage of our citizens take an active role to protect and improve their community and their nation, even to take time to vote.

Let us fairly and realistically ask ourselves some questions. Have we developed into a nation where some want to enjoy power just for prestige and benefits? Are government representatives more devoted to an undefined and fickle political party than to national needs and the general welfare? If the reaction to these questions tends to be in the affirmative then we must challenge ourselves to seek some significant changes in our governmental machinery to meet the demands of the 21st century. Every day that goes by and with each passing year when no significant improvement is made in our republic we will see its meaning and effectiveness lessened, its cause depleted and "that government of the people, by the people and for the people" will indeed perish from the earth.

A government by, for and of the people as well as a moral society has an obligation to protect its citizens from any and all intrusions whether that intrusion is a terrorist, a burglar or a thief parading as a merchant. The people at large have a right to protect themselves against the loss of the necessities of life – clean air, clean water and uncontaminated earth. Human health is a national necessity – an essential ingredient to the pursuit of happiness. Education is an economic and political necessity. Both are required to promote the general welfare.

If democracy is to be made real and permanent then the obstacles must be confronted and that elusive ideal of promoting the general welfare will need to be instilled into every phase of the public order as an imminent feature of our social mores. We should never underestimate the strength, internal peace and contentment that results from compassion and ethical conduct. A society grows great and strong through such deportment.

People don't rise from nothing. We owe something to parenting and patronage. The people who stand before kings may look like they did it all by themselves. But in fact they are invariably the beneficiaries of hidden advantages and extraordinary opportunities and cultural legacies that allow them to learn and work hard and make sense of the world in ways others cannot. It makes a difference where and when we grow up. The culture we belong to and the legacies passed down by our forebears shape the patterns of our achievements in ways we cannot begin to imagine.

Outliers, Malcolm Gladwell

CHAPTER 7

Secure the Blessings of Liberty to Ourselves and to our Posterity

"I'd like a country in which there was a maximum of opportunity for any individual to discover his talents and develop his capacities – discover his fullest self and by so doing learn to respect other selves a little." Robert P. Warren

This last of the six articles of the preamble made good on the "unalienable" right proclaimed in the Declaration of Independence as a "self-evident" truth. Its meaning involves an all-inclusive connotation summarizing the others and becomes a directive and purpose to preserve, maintain and improve our republic. From this directive we could surmise that our forefathers realized that the future would require amendments and corrections to accomplish what they had proposed. Recall that they had no previous model to direct them; they were crafting something new in the long history of mankind!

When their draft was completed, virtually all of the delegation harbored some doubts, some exceptions, regarding the final draft which they had proposed but only three delegates refused to sign. However, the delegation was certain of one thing, they had done their best. They were keenly aware that what they were offering was an experiment – an experiment to establish a republic to ensure those "unalienable" rights for which eighteen of the signers had fought a war to obtain. It would be up to the people to see if they could keep it. That was the injunction they imposed – we are now in custody of their direction – can we do it?

Future generations were therefore provided a means to make amendments as time and circumstances would undoubtedly require. The framers were trying to look ahead into an unknown future. The signers of the draft Constitution were experienced, practical men and realizing that their draft was not perfect, provided not only a method to amend it but they left also a blueprint of a republic in the preamble! The cause of liberty and the blessings it can bring to mankind were the underlying causes for the War of Independence. It is our duty to secure it.

Safety, liberty, equality and justice – words describing what people have yearned for over the ages, fought and died for and are the words which delineate the broad outlines of a republic. With security, liberty becomes most central since people with security and liberty will demand justice and when there is security, liberty and justice there will be social equality also. Together these blessings develop opportunities for the intellect, vision and determination of mankind. However, these blessings carry with them problems and obstacles as well, some antisocial characteristics seemingly ingrained in our nature, which require explicit laws and regulations in order to protect the social order. Responsible citizenship recognizes these obligations and utilizes liberty for personal advantages as well as enhancing the general welfare. "Liberty may be endangered by abuses of liberty as by the abuses of power." Federalist Papers, XLIII.

To secure the blessings of liberty imposes a host of obligations and responsibilities on the individual citizen, on society, on business and on government. How each constituent part fulfills its obligations, will influence the others and determine how the blessings of liberty will be realized by all of us.

The individual must understand and accept that liberty is not an unqualified right. It carries with it as an integral part, a responsibility to honor the same right to all others. It, therefore, is not a license to do as one pleases but is a right to pursue one's own goals and dreams in an ethical and charitable manner. Each person must respect the rights of others to their liberty otherwise there would be no liberty for anyone. No one can be given liberty to deny or infringe on the liberty of others except as punishment for crimes against society. The individual must, therefore, exercise liberty responsibly and with consideration of its consequences for the rights of others and, of vital importance, for the kind of society we live in.

If individual liberty is to exist in society it will have to observe limitations, it must be understood and employed responsibly. Ensuring liberty becomes a moral and ethical duty to be a good neighbor. In so doing, even in small ways, when and where it is needed and as we are able, a consequential step is taken toward a better neighborhood, city, state and nation. We thereby advance the cause of liberty. A question must be posed to every citizen: do you take from society more than you add to it? Is our mission in life to leave things a little better than what it would have been without us? It is easy to see why Thomas Jefferson insisted that education was the key to a republic – and to a society that will secure the blessings of our liberty.

How society encourages, supports and exercises liberty exemplifies a vital part of our social mores and reveals the kind of people we are. Personal liberty exercised responsibly becomes a blessing to mankind which our forefathers understood and therefore intended it to be a directive of government to ensure. But personal liberty gone amok in society challenges the bounds of democratic tolerance. It threatens public safety, public health, morality and general welfare. Human fallibility therefore results in the necessity for laws to set boundaries on individual and social activity, without which anarchy would prevail. What we do and permit in society becomes the ultimate driving force of our culture and of our nation.

Our mandate as citizens is to follow precepts of a republic whereby we must realize and acknowledge a requirement to exercise control over our government – a government which is our spokesman and ambassador! A true republic is like any growing and developing thing which will shrivel and become lethargic in the hands of duplicitous politicians who give little allegiance to the public. Whatever controls, statutes and regulations adopted by "our" government should be adopted only for purposes required for the general welfare and for society to function effectively, safely and harmoniously.

Government, according to true republican principles, should serve its citizens and those citizens have a corresponding right and duty to correct any errors, breach of faith or excessive use of delegated authority. This is how the blessings of liberty can be preserved. How much of this theory rings true today? How do members of Congress check with their constituency regarding critical legislation? Or do they check with party leaders and financial supporters? Do they conduct themselves as your representative or do they appear as your leader?

Every business enterprise has obligations and responsibilities in helping to secure the blessings of liberty just as all other members of society. Business practices must be in harmony with democratic principles in society. This involves a respect for the dignity of all employees and joint efforts in the determination of salaries, wages and working conditions. Obviously every business is unique in many respects and what works as an employee agreement in one business may not have application in another. Equally obvious is the necessity for every business to be profitable as well as providing reasonable employee benefits. Agreement on all these issues requires an honest, open and respectful deliberation between and among all parties concerned.

Equally important is that every business enterprise must exhibit a social conscience by respecting public health and safety and the life necessities to protect the air, water and soil. As a quid pro-quo every business enterprise can make use of various public amenities and services as well as a labor market. Additionally certain public projects and special amenities to promote and enhance private enterprise are always in order as long as it is done with open, visible public awareness and is a positive addition to the public welfare.

A free people in a republic therefore have the duty and are charged to play a managing and determining role to ensure liberty through governmental action. This requires intelligent and informed determinations in the selection of true representatives, to establish boundaries for human conduct and to demand and guarantee basic and fundamental human rights in society. These constitutional and legal guarantees to protect liberty and to criminalize those actions which deny liberty are inherent duties of representative government.

Every liberty which one person is free to exercise must be available to all others. These liberties may pertain to choices of personal lifestyles, to individual rights of choice, to the right to vote, to secure an education, to voice their opinions, to expect justice, opportunity and to receive needed healthcare. Consider the comment of Will Rogers," You contact your state or the federal government that your cow or hog is sick and they will send out experts from Washington and appropriate money to eradicate the cause. You wire them that your baby has diphtheria or scarlet fever and see what they do…..Why can't we get a government to at least do for a child's protection, what they do for a cow or a hog?"

The health care of each individual is a protection of public health in society. How many people have been unable to have the life they may have had due to an inability to afford the health care they required – from prenatal, babyhood on into young adulthood? How many potentially great people have we lost? Healthcare becomes a fundamental human right in a republic and must be ensured through appropriate governmental action. Virtually every industrialized nation in the world provides universal health care. Is it not obvious that the good health of people, public enterprise and social progress will predict the blessings of liberty? Will the same combination enhance our representative form of government? Will the same combination strengthen our nation?

Liberty is a blessing and obviously well worth ensuring. But liberty is also a challenge. It is a challenge faced by a free society which places on each of its citizens an obligation always to use the better side of our nature. How do you exercise that obligation? This is a question all of us must answer. Some members of society may wish to emphasize self-indulgence, pleasure seeking or other hedonistic practice. Others may place their preferences toward some form of public service, developing a business, or some profession. The possibilities are numerous and varied covering all areas of human interests and activity. Liberty is opportunity – an indispensable blessing or anathema.

What we must guard against is misunderstanding or misusing liberty. There seems to be nothing which someone cannot corrupt, defile or in some way use in ways for which it was never intended. Regardless of the career, profession or calling there is a need for guides, standards and legal safeguards. For wherever people are required to perform any service or duty there must be well defined rules and/or procedures governing its performance and some method to prevent antisocial practices or use. Only in Utopia can people live without rules!

An interesting development in "our" society is the formation of classes. To some degree, this feature has always been with us but it has become more pronounced in recent years. The use of terms such as "upper-class", "middle-class" and "lower class" are blithely used in newspapers, magazines, radio and television. Political leaders use these terms also. Somewhat amazingly most people seem to place themselves in one of these classes usually using income and wealth as the criteria.

This development is a subtle disparagement to the legal concept of equality, and to liberty. There is no biological foundation to substantiate this development; it is based primarily on material wealth and a birthright. Does it mean that we, as a nation, have become comfortable and now accept that there are natural and acceptable dividing differences among us based upon our wealth? We hear from all media sources references to citizens as "ordinary" citizens. These circumstances, hopefully, have not been intended to disparage "typical" citizens but rather have become commonly accepted dialogue that distinguishes between those who have public acclaim and those who don't. It is not a feature that fits or enhances the quality of human liberty, legal or social equality and certainly not compatible with securing the blessings of liberty.

Taken together, social stratification and subtle references to equality, become public mindsets, and of much more danger is the mindset of "our representatives". It is a mindset which tends to establish a converse hierarchy where those who are elected to serve become elevated above the public, which they are meant to serve. In a republic we are all "typical" or "regular" citizens and representatives need to be mindful of their obligations to serve and render meaningful public service. The way people think of, and speak of, various matters symbolize belief and belief can easily transform into overt action. We should never ignore nor minimize these seemingly mindless denigrations of the general public and the dignity and equality of humanity.

Most people will argue that such developments are "just the way things are" and many will insist that it is the inevitable result of the differences in people. This latter position is usually based on the premise that some people are naturally superior and, therefore, deserve to be at the top of the social ladder. But as we have seen earlier in this treatise there are multiple reasons for this situation where the factors of equal education, equal healthcare, equal opportunity, safe and secure neighborhoods and an improved value system can result in a great equalizer. This will bring us to a greater realization and respect of and for liberty as well as recognizing the essence of humanity – their dignity.

As youngsters many, if not most of us, were taught to honor, respect and, to some extent glorify, our founding ancestors. We marveled at the astonishing determination and sacrifices of those volunteer soldiers at Valley Forge and the bravery displayed throughout the War for Independence. We were amazed and proud of our constitutional framers for their intelligence, their foresight and the legacy of liberty which they left for us.

When we grew older we came to realize that those people were much like us. They were faced with different problems and life was not easy for them for they faced a totally different environment from what we have known. The environment they faced presented them with a choice to accept subjugation under a tyrant King and to forgo personal liberty or fight for those self-evident truths which our Creator endowed us. They chose to fight!

Today we live in a vastly new environment. We are no longer threatened to be subjugated by a king but by a much more insidious and designing antagonist – it is the way we have allowed our social and economic way of life to develop without thought or design. Machiavelli could not have dreamed of a more clever ploy than what we have developed without meaning to do it – a pseudo democratic oligarchy. This has developed as result of the ability of powerful lobbies having free access to the people's representatives in order to insert their operational exemptions and subsidies into the law of the land.

In our free society this has resulted in several international corporations and individuals to garner massive wealth far beyond reasonable needs or requirements. Such massive wealth has been elevated to be the real driving force in our society. This success is often applauded without thinking or considering how this wealth came about, where or from whom it came or what economic consequences would result. This is not new in our society. Will Rogers, nearly a century ago noted the same thing, pointing out that we publicized the winners but gave no consideration or thought to those from whom it was derived.

Neither Will Rogers nor this writer points out this situation to stigmatize those with great wealth but rather to sound an alarm regarding a system with few meaningful guidelines and rules regarding fair and honest practice in our business, governmental and financial institutions. As President James Madison reminded us, "If men were angels no government would be necessary." Yes, without a doubt, government is necessary to preserve the blessings of liberty.

This isn't a matter of legal regulations only; it is a matter of social and economic consequences. Each of us is a member of society and what we do has an effect on others. How each of us behaves and conducts ourselves has an impact on society as a whole – for good or for bad. This is why there must be rules and limits placed on all actions and practices whether they relate to individual conduct, political conduct or economic conduct.

If a "blame game" is to be voiced, don't point to the wealthy; don't vent your objections too loudly toward the politician because the fault lands on all of us. First, we, as citizens, have neglected our duty to demand appropriate representation, and we have largely ignored what has been happening; second, by becoming an automatic and favorable vote when the candidate is from the party of choice regardless of issues or the candidate's record or competency; and third, by not joining or supporting efforts to correct a broken system of representation and how political campaigns have become managed by politicians and special interests. All of these refer to duties of citizenship in a republic. How many of us would be graded well by this test?

If we are really intent on securing the blessings of liberty it is essential to realize and accept the fact that liberty, like all things, has limits. No one has liberty to devise or utilize personal or public advantages which are not openly available and accessible to everyone. No one has liberty to deprive or deny liberty to any law-abiding person. No one has a right to deny any person of anything of value without providing an equal, acceptable return. These are matters of personal and social morality.

It will be possible to achieve a better, fairer and more enjoyable social and economic balance only through universal education and by reforming our representative governmental system to be responsible to the public only – by eliminating all of the "middlemen". The great educational, intellectual divide must be addressed by examining all parts of our social order – parenting, universal education, neighborhood environments and attention by knowledgeable, responsible public representatives. Our social habits and activities, our economy and our very survival as a free society depend on it.

Ongoing programs, not sporadic initiatives, are indispensable elements for a solution which requires contributions from all sources of society. If the situation is left unattended it could develop into a contest between a republic and an ochlocracy where mobs or gangs hold the reins of the social order each in their own little domain. When we witness International drug cartels, street gangs and Mafia type organizations we should realize the necessity to put in practice ideas and programs to develop a political and social order conducive to education, safety and progress, all geared toward enjoying the blessings of liberty. A social system cannot be coerced. It is only through concerted personal and public action based on intelligent public programs, that over time, we can achieve positive results.

We, in our time, must fully realize that liberty is tied to and depends upon an authentic representative government. A lackadaisical and uninvolved citizenry is a very favorable and suitable candidate to be taken advantage of by any of the numerous power seekers who look for just the right opportunity. We can all contribute to securing the blessings of liberty by taking an active part in public affairs by considering the issues and candidates without being a "taken for granted voter". If we demand true representation, fair elections in political campaigns, a truly independent and qualified judiciary, a world class educational system, and promote social values in harmony with all these constituent parts we will have taken actions to secure the blessings of liberty for ourselves, to our posterity and beyond.

Plato's political philosophy rests upon his principles that the individual is more important than society and that it is necessary to know the nature of individuals in order to ascertain the characteristics of a desirable society. The good society depends upon virtuous persons, and virtue depends upon the character of individual citizens. It is not necessarily the system of society itself which creates evil social conditions, but it is the individuals who populate it. Good people produce a good state, while corrupt people engender corrupt politics.*

*Ideas of the Great Philosophers
William S. Sahakian
Mabel Lewis Sahakian

Chapter 8

Our Bill of Liberty

"The open-mind never acts; when we have done our utmost to arrive at a reasonable conclusion, we still, when we can reason and investigate no more, must close our minds for the moment with a snap, and act dogmatically on our conclusions. George Bernard Shaw, Androcles and the Lion

It is important to capitalize on the lessons we can learn from mistakes and shortcomings of past civilizations which alert us to our own imperfections. Failures of past empires encompass many causes. Typically the factors which dictated national policy involved lust for power, fame and wealth together with misguided and exaggerated concepts of self-worth. People, obsessed with ambition, pursued personal desires and ignored national interests. We have witnessed envy and hatred between vying parties, each determined to gain control without regard to consequences. Society faces a long and difficult journey to improve the conduct, attitude and perspectives of humankind but serious contemplation, application of our national intelligence and an honest desire for improvement can, and has yielded great results.

Is it possible that we, in our time, have become so accustomed to talking about our republic that we have accepted it as fact without questioning its veracity? A completely unbiased observer would tell us that we have the governmental structure but our practice negates the premise. Our

Constitution established a form of representation which fit conditions in 1789. Today, two and a quarter centuries later, five counties in California have more population than the entire 13 original colonies and are the equivalent to eight of our smallest states!

The very definition of a republic requires representation of people, not land. In addition, the intrusion of hundreds of millions of dollars into political campaigns distorts any idea of governmental rule by people – democracy. When we insert gerrymandered congressional districts, restriction of voting rights, manipulation of ballots, special privileges and exemptions and a host of other acts of political chicanery, no one could claim they have described a republic. We may be better defined as a pseudo-democratic oligarchy!

It is time for a new Bill of Rights, a Bill of Liberty – to save the Republic of the United States. Some possibilities are submitted as a starting point.

I. Elections of all federal officials should be governed by federal regulations and should be regulated on a non-partisan basis. Every citizen of the United States, who is 18 years of age or over, properly registered, should be eligible to vote based on identification specified by federal law.

II. The president and vice president should be elected by direct vote of the people.

III. No state should have more senators than congressmen. The value of each senator's vote should be based upon the proportion of the state population compared to the total national population. Senators should be limited to four terms and members of the House of Representatives should be limited to five terms. Terms for members of the House of Representatives should be four years with one-half of the membership terms coinciding with presidential elections. All members of the House of Representatives should be elected on a statewide basis.

IV. All political campaigns should be limited to 65 days prior to the date of election. All qualifying candidates should receive public financing and no private funds should be used by any candidate. All qualified candidates for any federal office should be required to submit a verified personal resume and application for the office which he or she seeks. No candidate should be eligible for political office who has signed or otherwise agreed to do or not to do anything other than supporting his/her position on public issues openly expressed.

V. All political parties should be nationally incorporated and required to conform to guidelines as specified by law including a requirement to file biennial platforms stating their fundamental beliefs and their position on current issues. All parties should pledge to utilize only verified information for all political advertising.

VI. All television and radio stations conducting interstate business should carry a minimum of three debates of no less than 90 uninterrupted minutes for presidential elections and one such debate for Senatorial and House of Representatives elections at no public cost.

VII. A bipartisan select committee representing both the Senate and House, approved by a two thirds vote of both houses, should be established to counsel with the President and Secretary of State in the development and conduct of foreign relations and national defense. Foreign relations should be designated as a nonpartisan activity.

VIII. The Supreme Court should consist of 12 members appointed by the president through a merit system as approved by the United States Senate. Rulings of unconstitutionality of laws duly passed by the Congress and approved by the president should be by a two thirds vote of the total membership of the court. The court should be relocated from Washington DC to a central location with consideration given to both population and geographical criteria.

IX. Congress should pass comprehensive legislation requiring the equal protection of all laws of the United States to apply to all people in all public and commercial activities with no exceptions. No law should grant any special privilege or right to any person, group or commercial interest unless the public interest is served thereby and approved by two thirds majority of each house. No salary should be paid to any member of Congress until appropriate legislation is enacted to provide for these two requirements.

X. Every citizen of the United States should have an unqualified right to a public education from preschool through high school. Provisions should be established to effectuate this right prior to adjournment of the first Congress following the adoption of this amendment. No charge should be required for admission or attendance through high school and all required books and school supplies should be furnished equally to all students.

A prescription for life as responsible human beings is to leave things better than they were when we arrived. This becomes a valid formula for the advancement of humanity. This is now our time and the lives of future generations will be influenced and impacted by what we do or what we failed or neglected to do. These are defining days not only for our nation but perhaps the greatest chance for all people all over the world to be able to continue to see and to know that the beacon of freedom lives on. Our republic is doomed to failure only if good, fair and well-meaning people do nothing.

"Man did not enter society to be worse off, or to have fewer rights, but rather to have those rights better secured."* Hopefully we are a society which will seriously reflect on these issues and proposals and where social groups, non-partisan in composition and purpose, will come

---

*   "Common Sense", Thomas Paine

together all over the land to take up the issues and press for answers to revitalize our ailing republic. "Those who expect to reap the blessings of freedom must undergo the fatigues of supporting it." **

"We must forget what is behind. If we cease to originate, we are lost, we can only keep what we have, by new activity."***

** Ibid
*** "The Crown Treasury of Relevant Quotations." Edward F Murphy, quoting William Ellery Channing, from "Doctor Channing's Notebook."

Among the most formidable of the obstacles which the new Constitution will have to encounter may readily be distinguished the obvious interest of a certain class of men in every state to resist all changes which may hazard a diminution of the power, emolument, and consequence of the offices they hold under the state establishments; and the perverted ambition of another class of men, who will either hope to aggrandize themselves ..... (and) the honest errors of minds led astray by preconceived jealousies and fears.

Publius – The Federalist I

EPILOGUE

"when the group or a civilization declines, is through no mystic limitation of a corporate life, but through the failure of its political or intellectual leaders to meet the challenge of change." Will and Ariel Durrant

Is the United States worth saving? The answer is a resounding yes –but not as a pseudo-democratic oligarchy designed to give preferential treatment to a few who have the means to manipulate the system for personal gain; not for a government which deceives the public by presenting itself as a democracy while being financially promoted by well-placed entities, individual and corporate; and not for a plutocracy or a theocracy. It is only a true republic dedicated to our founding values that is worth saving and fighting for. For this we can rededicate ourselves to put in place those fundamental protections which will prove to the world that a true republic can endure.

The United States is a great nation, the greatest nation in the world. But do we desire this greatness based only on our military power and the abundance of natural resources? Or do we prefer to be a land where people, all the people, can live together in civilized harmony promoting liberty, safety, justice and opportunity for the benefit of everyone. Our greatness must be judged and exemplified by the living conditions of all of our citizens so that other nations can view the capability of a free people.

The course of humanity for centuries to come may rest on how we, by our example, illustrate to the world how people can govern themselves – that a society composed of the world's people can manage their government. All our lives we have pledged allegiance to a government which stands for human equality and liberty. The time has come to show by action, not by oratory, that we mean what we say. Our failure will result in the loss of the greatest test of democracy which the world has ever witnessed.

What should we expect from government? Human institutions will never be perfect but certainly we should insist on honest and capable efforts to protect, defend and enhance our safety, to secure a proficient justice system, to safeguard equal opportunity, to ensure that laws and regulations are fair and apply equally to everyone and always to seek to develop that more perfect union.

When we are faced with flawed election practices, overly ambitious zealots rendering negotiations on critical national issues impracticable, the picture becomes clear that unbending political rivalry makes realistic compromises impossible. The entire nation suffers when such a stalemate occurs. The people's government becomes ungovernable, just as our first president warned. The fundamental question becomes how to define the essential requirements for democracy. The answers are embedded in a clear understanding of what liberty is and what it isn't, what responsible public representation demands and the provision for a first-class public education system.

What is liberty? Liberty in a republic entails an unfettered right to think, and responsibly act to promote oneself toward any goal or way of life which does not restrict or deny the same latitude and options to anyone else. The antithesis to liberty is to always insist while being unwilling to accept any idea, goal or objective which is contrary to one's preferred position. Liberty requires more altruism and less selfishness.

Education in a free society entails development of a factual understanding that all people are the same in their fundamental wants and needs as well as in their genetic makeup; that they are diversified only by tens of thousands of years of separation and the resultant requirements for survival and environmental effects. Education entails an understanding of the world we live in; how a better society can be developed and each person's responsibilities to make it so. Education not only requires knowledge and skills to make a living, how to be a productive member of society, but also how to manage a representative government.

The aspirations of our constitutional framers for a republic were intended to achieve what humankind has striven for throughout history. From our beginnings as an essentially Anglo-Saxon heritage we have become a nation representative of the world's peoples – we are called Americans. As such we have developed our own unique culture based on the prospects for liberty and opportunity. However, in our exuberance to capitalize on this liberty and opportunity have we neglected to improve our collective behavior which shapes society, the economy and our government? Have we made timely and effective responses to change, growth and new circumstances? Have we given purposeful attention to the quality and direction of our society? Have we forgotten that our nation is unique?

It is our social mores and our determination to preserve our founding values that in the long term, will determine whether we succeed in self-government! To save the United States we must realize that culture is learned, embracing its customs, attitudes, behavior and beliefs. It is parenting, neighborhood environments and early education which are basic in determining the quality of life of people and eventually the quality of our governance.

It requires only a brief inspection of the characteristics and circumstances of our society and our government to lead us to some answers as to whether our republic is achieving its principal aims and purpose. In today's America we find that about one percent who are able to live like ancient monarchs, we find many who do exceptionally well and many more that live adequately. At the same time however we find far too many who live at or near a meager subsistence level and an even greater number who live in abject poverty.

At the same time we see an ever-growing trend toward class distinctions. At the same time we witness an ever-growing development where cloistered groups, designed for political interests, dogmatically insisting on their way in spite of being out of touch with national interests. We should have been adequately warned that unfamiliarity with history makes us destined to repeat it.

Other threats to democracy have evolved in the form of rigged election districts, and an economy which has become more and more internationally owned or controlled by multinational syndicates along with some foreign governments. None of these portray republican principles as their business model. Characteristics and situations of this nature should make it clear that we must install new measures to reinvent our society and adopt new constitutional guarantees to preserve free popular government.

The only way for meaningful corrections to occur is for the public to demand it – not for any ideology but for the sake of public safety, liberty, justice and opportunity. If the voice of the public rises to the occasion it will happen – a unified voice of the public becomes a power that cannot be resisted. When the people control their government they will have no fear of that government – provided one is willing to abide by responsible majority rule and social justice.

When national security is threatened due to warfare, economic depression or widespread national disasters or epidemics, there will be no clamor about states' rights but only a willingness and realization that it is only by a beneficial response as a unified nation which can maintain our greatness and security in a growing and threatening world. It will only become "our" government when it is controlled by all the people through authentic elections.

We must learn from history and accept the many warnings it teaches. Let us not repeat the mistakes over and over again. History clearly shows that monarchies, as a form of social and political organization, have prevailed longer than any other form of government. It did this through the force of arms, cultural belief connecting government with religion – the divine rights of Kings – and was perpetuated due to the ignorance of uneducated masses of people. With the exception of relatively short periods of time monarchies never achieved real beneficial results for the human condition. Instead, they brought on more misery for the general public who were essentially slaves in a class divided society.

Historically, republican rule has depended upon an oligarchy – led by an aristocracy and/or a dominant religion which "allowed" a semblance of public control and participation and through such deceit perpetuated themselves. Our own government was created and initially operated in a vaguely similar fashion. The right to vote was narrowly defined. Our constitutional framers were very leery of the common man as being capable of running a true democracy. This is why our early presidents insisted on education of the general public as a means of preserving a republic.

Jean Jacques Rousseau [1712 – 1778] the French social reformer and philosopher, maintained that it was "unnatural" for the majority of a nation's people to manage government. He thought that a small minority should manage an oligarchic republic. The small group, he envisioned, would be intellectually capable and socially minded enough that they would govern for the benefit of all. It was a paternalistic concept which viewed the general public as too uneducated to participate in government. Should we depend upon those in power to always do what is right for everyone unless there are specific rules and parameters on actions to prescribe the way? Does 18th-century thinking still survive?

Earlier in this treatise there is a reference to Charles Luis Montesquieu [1689 – 1755] who considered that a true republic ruled by the people, could only exist over time if the society was small and homogeneous in race and religion. So far, after 2¼ centuries we would have to say that President James Monroe was right in his rebuttal that in a country with much diversity, there would have to be a democracy so that all positions on all issues could voice their opinions and be considered. Note that he used the word "considered" and not "totally accepted". Does this sound like referencing a need for compromise? This illustrates why education becomes vital – our republic depends on it! Although our nation has suffered the calamity of a civil war, we still cling to the idea that we are Americans first and foremost, the only government of its kind in the history of the world!

History also tells us that some among us would only want to rule, not to lead; it points to the innate fallibility of our nature; it tells us that we, the people, have a strong tendency to repeat ourselves and have a hard time learning to accept what history teaches. The lesson to be learned is that we must adapt to changing times and conditions and use our intelligence to determine and act on what we know is right for our time. History clearly illustrates what people are prone to do; their collective actions tend to repeat their mistakes. The history of governments also teaches that fundamental legal guarantees must be in place to direct and control governmental practice.

This extremely encapsulated reference to history is to remind us that the government we live under is unique in the long history of mankind – it is an exception in history and only a unified public with determination can it be maintained. History points to the undeniable fact that governments have rarely lasted much longer than ours. Some might say that only the old Roman Empire lasted longer but it should be noted that that Empire went through many changes and alterations during its long history. Historians agree that governments go through cycles and that they have a beginning, they flower and then they decline and become replaced. We must ask ourselves if our internal will has been depleted by our over indulgence and misuse of liberty or have we maintained the nerve and resolve of our forefathers to make the fundamental changes required to preserve liberty in the 21st century – or has "our" republic been replaced already?

For more than a century this nation has been moving steadily toward a government which grants favors to a select few – those who have meaningful access to government officials and regulators. This trend has become commonplace while receiving minimal attention by the general public or being exposed by the media. This process is still continuing behind the scenes like an invisible authority usurping the liberties which this nation was created to provide.

This is usually accomplished in the name of free enterprise. The peril comes from deluding the public by disguising many of these activities as capitalism in order to gain public acceptance as if they represent free competitive enterprise. Free competitive enterprise is completely unrelated to this kind of arrangement and is actually defiled by such practice. True competitive enterprises now face a do or die situation against international conglomerates.

A slow, creeping and unobtrusive invasion into democratic procedures and rights receives only sporadic questioning and soon becomes positioned in the culture of our nation, especially in Washington DC, as the accepted norm, It seems to be human nature to quickly dismiss and forget what seem to be only slight offenses which have little immediate public impact. But when these infractions to democratic processes accumulate over a century or more they become a tidal wave that destroys the very foundation of the republic. When the general public and the media refuse or neglect to pay close attention to their government they are guilty of allowing the liberties and rights of everyone to be eroded.

Our "civilization" as restricted to the United States of America, has developed its own culture, its unique social order, which must be protected by a justice system and directed by a government which the people must insist upon being one of our own choosing – selection of representatives by citizens' ballots, not by campaign financing. It is a civilization and culture which will demand and achieve its goal of a true republic or it will decay and become an oligarchy under the yoke of economic power and take its place in the graveyard of other failed governments.

We are now perilously close to the end game where the people become "very ordinary" citizens and that great unsuspecting public – will descend into a permanent "lower-class" which has always been necessary to serve and maintain those few (1% or 2% of the total population) powerful and ultra-wealthy families. This is a scene reminiscent of middle-age monarchy which presents some frightful comparisons to several aspects of modern-day America.

Everyone desires a comfortable and carefree existence but when a disproportionate amount of a nation's income and wealth is acquired by a relative few, it will never translate into a healthy and robust national economy or to the overall improvement of society. Such a condition becomes an aberration of what a democracy in a civilized society should produce or tolerate. Achieving a better balance is what is worth saving and fighting for but can only happen when we reinvigorate our founding values, establish a world class educational system opened to everyone and free our representatives from special interest controls.

Faithfully dedicated public representatives will applaud this possibility so that they can serve our country and the vast public who deserve it. If the present trend is not corrected soon and our justice system should ever evolve into conformity with the economic trends, our hopes for a true republic will vanish leaving no hope of redemption against the massive influence and power of the new aristocracy.

If we minimize or scoff at the reality of our present situation we need only to look at some specific incidents that occur and continue uncorrected. Look at a Supreme Court decision, seemingly based on doctrinaire ideology, which recently invented a new person –they turned a legal fabrication, called a corporation, into a human being, with the same legal rights to perform financially in electing our representatives the same as a "fellow citizen". This is a situation which begs for correction so that our representatives can do the job which they are elected to do, represent real people, actual life forms called citizens of the United States. Few representatives, if any, desire to be beholden to an international conglomerate, some national corporation or a wealthy gambler.

Citizen efforts should always be to make right what is wrong, to make what is unfair, fair. In order to do this it becomes necessary that legal protections must be in place to guard against dishonest and unethical practices in all public affairs – the removal of temptation is a great aid for honest behavior. Our efforts must be to equalize opportunity, reform governmental organization and practice, in order to better guarantee public representation and strive to live in a just and more humanitarian society.

Difficult economic times tend to bring out a more ignoble side of many of those who are or feel their welfare and safety threatened. Keep in mind that safety – survival – is the strongest of all human emotions and even liberty will be sacrificed to achieve it. When people are threatened economically they will tend to look at others as being the reason for their misfortune and will become resentful of them. It is prone to develop confrontations of the private sector versus public sector, union versus nonunion, rich versus poor and large numbers versus immigrants who are perceived as the problem.

Rather than uniting to solve the real problems, a common instinct is to search for a scapegoat. When large numbers of citizens take this course of action, meaningful action becomes extremely difficult to achieve and many people are inclined to take hard and fast positions with an unfailing conviction of the validity of their opinions only. Resentment, frustration and suspicion become giant roadblocks to solutions and the root causes of problems get lost when most action becomes development of strategy to achieve one's uncompromising way.

An angry and frustrated public becomes easy prey for demagogues whose only mission is to gain power, prominence and be elected or reelected. This is why the typical citizen needs a valid method to evaluate the resume of all candidates who propose to lead us and political parties need to be accountable for their proclaimed agendas.

This is a time which tests our ability, our resolve and our devotion to self-government and will determine whether we will lead or we will be led. In a republic this is the only choice; it never was and never can be both ways. The answer, in words, is easy – do we choose to preserve liberty or do we ignore that choice and submit to whatever an unseen authority may choose to give us? Which will be your choice? Are there any of us today who would repeat and believe what Patrick Henry said – give me liberty or give me death?

Our lives are limited and each generation is another link in the chain of human existence. What will our contribution be toward a better society and a more perfect union? Whether that contribution is positive or negative, it will have a great impact upon the lives of our children and our grandchildren and beyond. Shall we have that great satisfaction, pride and joy of being the ones to reinvent and make secure a true republic for ourselves, for posterity and for the people of the world? You are the one that must provide the answer.

www.ingramcontent.com/pod-product-compliance
Lightning Source LLC
Chambersburg PA
CBHW052137110526
44591CB00012B/1762